REFLECTIONS

for the

GOLDEN

YEARS

Angela Macnamara

First published 2005 by
Veritas Publications
7/8 Lower Abbey Street
Dublin 1
Ireland
Email publications@veritas.ie
Website www.veritas.ie

ISBN 1 85390 886 X

10 9 8 7 6 5 4 3 2 1

Acknowledgement
A number of the quotations heading each chapter are to be
found in *Age Doesn't Matter Unless You're a Cheese* by Kathryn and
Ross Petras (Workman Publishing, New York).

A catalogue record for this book
is available from the British Library.

Printed in the Republic of Ireland
by
Betaprint Ltd, Dublin

Veritas books are printed on paper made from the wood
pulp of managed forests. For every tree felled, at least one
tree is planted, thereby renewing natural resources.

CONTENTS

THE

IMPORTANCE

OF

REMAINING ACTIVE

CHAPTER 1

OPEN TO NEW IDEAS

'THE CLOSING YEARS OF LIFE ARE LIKE THE END OF A
MASQUERADE PARTY, WHEN THE MASKS ARE DROPPED'.

Arthur Schopenhauer

It was windy outside with squally rain. I was in the hall tying one of those plastic rain bonnets on my head. I had always thought of them as being for old women when I realised, 'Hey! That's me now'. In my seventies I can relax and take on the plastic head-gear, not caring if it's unfashionable. At least it will save me from looking like a 'whirling dervish' when I arrive at my destination. There is little possibility of looking attractively windswept when you are over seventy.

That started me thinking about writing down some of the experiences and thoughts about getting older as I am actually living those years. There is no period in life that does not have its own silver lining. We can often feel ten years or more younger as we set about some task or hobby. Other times I find myself asking, 'Is this old lady actually ME?' And she is. I, who had for so long been wrapped up in life with family, work and social commitments, am now a free agent and it can feel like standing naked, swept in on a new beach – something of a beached whale. I have to clothe myself anew, redesign my life. Perhaps I have ten more years, maybe less. People tell me that one is inclined to define old age as being ten years older than one is oneself.

I remember the first time I landed with a dull *clunk* having jumped off a low wall while on a country walk. I was about sixty and it was the first time I understood the meaning of losing the spring from one's step. It wasn't long after that when I began to occasionally forget the names of people and places; it seems that names are one of the first games the memory plays with ageing. 'Join the club', was the wry comment of a friend. Laughingly, she told me that such lapses of memory were humorously referred to as 'senior moments', thus conferring them with a certain dignity.

Retirement leaves us feeling a new freedom. This can feel like a glorious challenge as, at first, we see the silver lining. 'I can do whatever I want, whenever I like.' Now I can let go of false things. Freedom can also mean not having to live up to other people's expectations. No need to log onto the internet or send endless text messages unless that's what I choose to do. Many retired people are understandably daunted by the thought of computer technology. It becomes harder to take it in when some only start in their seventies. It's difficult not to worry when shops, hotels, organisations and media provide only 'dot com' addresses as the means of communicating with them. Let's put in a word for adding the old-fashioned telephone number and address for those of us who aren't familiar with the computer world. A friend of mine asked her twelve-year-old grandson to explain to her some of the magic of his computer with a view to her taking lessons. But he was such a whizz-kid at it that she felt her brain seize up with only one lesson. What we've never had we don't miss, she decided. Younger people do not understand that the brain takes new ideas in more slowly as one ages. Of course, there are brilliant people whose brains continue to be technologically sharp well into old, old age. I just manage the computer at the most basic level, only a little beyond word-processing, and I feel hassled if anyone tries to push me on into mysterious levels of techno-savvy.

Yet it would be all too easy for some of us to become – quite unnecessarily – couch potatoes, flicking around the TV channels for most of the day. But rather than be a lazy spud, each of us needs to look positively and realistically at what shape the rest of our life might take. Then, 'Go for it!' Let what you love deeply be realised.

Start early to develop interests and hobbies that you will still love when you are ninety.*

---

* Well worth buying is *The Retirement Book* by Anne Dempsey (published by the Recruitment Planning Council of Ireland) which provides invaluable advice on all aspects of retirement.

CHAPTER 2

FEELING FINE

'OLD AGE IS NOT FOR CRY-BABIES'

Bette Davis, Film Star

Somebody sent me the following little poem, entitled, 'I'm Fine, Thank You':

There is nothing the matter with me,
I'm as healthy as I can be.
Yes, I've arthritis in both my knees
And when I talk, I talk with a wheeze.
My pulse is weak and my blood is thin
But I'm awfully well for the shape I'm in.

Arch supports I have for my feet,
Or I wouldn't be able to trot up the street;
Sleep doesn't come easily all through the night,

But come the next morning I find I'm all
right.
My memory's wonky, my head tends to
swim –
But I'm awfully well for the shape I'm in.

The moral is this as my tale I unfold
That for you and for me who are coming
on old,
It's better to say 'I'm fine' with a grin,
Than to moan to the folks of the shape
we are in.

There are, of course, times when we have a
profound need to communicate pain and
anguish to a special friend or professional
helper. We may need to cry and to discover the
healing power of tears. But such deeply sharing
moments are not for casual social occasions.

Generally, it's good to have a laugh at
ourselves. Ageist attitudes tend to get absorbed
unknowingly. Yet we all know that at any age
there can be patches when we seem to have a
variety of aches and pains which prompt us to
think that a personal MOT (NCT) might be
timely! The fact of having a few chronic health

issues doesn't stop the majority of our 'good bits' from functioning really well. Indeed, people often speak of the compensations one gets for the loss of a particular sense. So it is important to focus on the areas in which all is still well. We have a challenge in continuing to do as well as possible those things we have always been able to handle. We may not be as swift in our movements as before but does that really matter? Younger people can be impetuous and, as in driving, go unnecessarily fast. But we calmly adjust the speed to suit the mind and body — plus the rules of the road. If you had a beloved pony who had pulled the family trap for many a year but has now grown old, you will notice that he slows to his own speed and you accept that with understanding. The old family dog drops some of his puppy-like tricks and finds himself a place in the sun. He and the pony are not given to fretting about their new situation. It doesn't preoccupy them or cause them to wonder what other ponies or dogs will think of their changed routine. How wise!

Of course, we too need to find the appropriate 'place in the sun' for ourselves as we get older. A comfortable chair is a special gift to oneself. But a comfortable frame of mind is a 'freebie' that is even more rewarding. Give yourself 'brownie points' for your on-going activities and for those out-going qualities of concern and care for others. Watch out for and behead any sign of disinterest in people and exaggerated self-pity. Regrets about past actions need to be left behind with the realisation that there is no changing them now. You had ups and downs. Today is the first day of the rest of your life. Like the pony and the dog, find activities you are comfortable with. Some may still climb up the nearest mountain. Others prefer to ford the stream or sit on the bank with toes in the water. Choice, freedom and responsibility are blessings.

These can be happy days of growth and creativity.

Look at the flowers: the daisy 'grows where it is planted'. It experiences from the outside, sunshine, storms, cold and warmth. It is buffeted by winds. Yet at its inner core is the strength to see all this as part of a daisy's experience and to accept it all as the harmony of life.

CHAPTER 3

DELVE INTO THE LIBRARY

'WORK IS A CREATIVE ADVENTURE.'

Paul Tournier

L ibraries are well worth visiting. In earlier years many busy people may not have used libraries fully: work and family filled their day. They bought books to read aloud to the family. Nowadays, the daily papers and current issues of magazines are available to read in the warmth of the quiet library. Computers are available to students. Not only do libraries have a multitude of books, but they also supply all sorts of facts about classes available for people of all ages. You will find that whatever art, craft, language or skill you wish to investigate, there is a class in your vicinity. There is also the possibility of your running an interesting class yourself if you have a particular skill which is not already catered for in the courses in a local school or adult education centre. So do go to the librarian and he or she will help you. Choose a time when they are not too busy dealing with a long queue at the counter. Then, when you have chosen your favourite subject look and see if there is a book on that topic in the library. It may be next term before you can get into a class or course so it is good to have read up a bit before that. Parish Active Retirement Associations, religious institutions and techs also have courses available for the elderly.*

Very often what we need is the will to take the first step. Many aspects of life may have become complicated for older people because of modern technology that can intimidate us. But fear not! You are going to be with other people around your own age when you do get as far as the class or course. The local library can be a gentle first step in the direction of a hobbies or further education class. Beginners are almost always catered for.

I understand that it was through the kind suggestion of the mother of ex-Taoiseach Charles Haughey, that we now qualify for free travel at the age of sixty-six. That opens wonderful possibilities for a trip into town for the day or even a day-trip taking a couple of hours on the train through the countryside, a nice meal and chat at one's destination and then the trip home. Also, if you are planning a holiday in the country it is a really encouraging start to be able to travel for free. God bless Mrs Haughey senior for that! Enquire at Bord Fáilte about discounts for older people available at some guest houses and B&Bs. An overnight spree can be such a pleasant change.

It's a very nice idea to buy a couple of tickets for a concert or theatre and invite a friend for this little treat. You can book by phone or internet and collect your ticket fifteen minutes before the entertainment starts. Look up the daily papers for the price of seats. No need to get the most expensive, but the cheapest may require that you have very good eyesight or the seats might be a bit hard. Try the middle range.

---

* Aontas, the National Association of Adult Education have about 3,000 courses available throughout the country.

The Retirement Planning Council of Ireland, which is a registered charity gives information on matters such as entitlements, finances, relationships, health in later years, use of time, etc. They also give Retirement Courses (charging a reasonable fee). Their address is 27-29 Lower Pembroke Street, Dublin 1. Telephone 01-6613139.

CHAPTER 4

CELEBRATE THE WISDOM YEARS

'EVEN IF A MOTHER FORGET THE CHILD OF HER WOMB, I SHALL NOT FORGET YOU.'

Isaiah 49:15-16

Creativity can broaden when we have the time and space in which to move on into new fields of experimentation. Some indomitable vintage people determine to celebrate their wisdom years. Dame Thora Hird and Mary Stott along with George Bernard Shaw continued to act, speak and write with consummate skill and good humour.

Then there are those who, in their seventies, assume that there is another job out there just waiting for them to come along. So they set out to search for it. They visit charitable organisations where voluntary help may be welcomed. Often, once installed in the job, they proceed to re-arrange the office or shop bringing their well-honed skills to bear on this new challenge and charming the customers in the process.

The old-agers who bravely step out and find a niche for themselves in the marketplace do not manage to avoid the wrinkles, stiff joints, failing sight or hearing which are part of our natural decline. They make up their minds to triumph over these. It is that spirit which marks them out as heroes. They are not going to allow themselves to be patronised. 'I can't "walk tall" physically any longer' said one octogenarian, 'but I'm damned if I'll allow that to bend my spirit.'

Those people who tend to be 'loners', can be happy loners. Extrovert people may pity the loner but he or she can be as busy as a bee within themselves. 'There are so many exciting thoughts to be thunk', enthused one such person. Reading, writing, studying, doing crosswords and communicating by letter – such activities fill their days. And then there are the gentle social occasions with friends and family with whom they feel completely at ease! 'Great not to have to change my pullover.'

I remember one well-known, well-travelled, well-off writer and socialite who castigated shy people who get anxious about social events. She thinks that they are self-absorbed and selfish. She says that everyone can feel nervous, but that some just get on with such social occasions. She, who would not need to introduce herself to anyone, advises that we all attend these gatherings and sail around introducing ourselves to all and sundry; easy for some. But not for the person with a shy nature and social anxiety. This person has usually had his or her confidence seriously undermined and has a real struggle to build self-esteem and confidence.

Yet it is true that we need to face the churning stomach and make an effort to keep going to smaller social events where there are fewer fearsomely extrovert people loudly and effusively greeting one another. It might be an advantage to all concerned if at business conferences or socials name-tags were compulsory. Forgetting people's names is one of the bugbears that could stop the shy person from venturing out.

On the other hand, there is the humourous old prayer that warns some of us:

> Keep me from the fatal habit of thinking that I must say something on every subject. Release me from the craving to straighten out somebody's affairs. Make me thoughtful but not moody: helpful but

not bossy. With my vast store of wisdom, it seems a pity not to use it all, but Thou knowest, Lord, that I want a few friends at the end...

CHAPTER 5

A MAKE-OVER

'COMPARING YOURSELF TO OTHERS IS ONE SURE ROUTE TO LOW SELF-ESTEEM.'

Self Esteem – The Lazy Person's Guide by Theresa Francis Cheung

We are links in a human chain and this involves responsibility, but not total sameness. A uniquely-shaped link can still hold the others together. People who want to be totally free may make a loud declaration of independence. As life goes on we come to realise that it is more truly human to make a declaration of *dependence*. We need one another and, indeed, we often depend on one another for our feelings of being okay. Yet it is also important that we stand, however shakily, on our own two feet, do our own thing insofar as we are able, link the arm of a friend when needed while remaining our unique selves.

None of us is exactly like anyone else. This is reflected interestingly in the fact that however great or small our homes may be, we all choose our own way of decorating and furnishing them. Most of us hope that family or friends will share our home happily, regularly or intermittently. Some leave the door open and depend on droppers-in for regular news and chat. Others are more private and appreciate a mixture of time alone and time shared. There are also those with a taste for solitude.

Whether or not we have guests or 'droppers-in', it is peace-inducing to keep the home looking warm and inviting. A vase of flowers, the smell of furniture polish – or of ironing – a cosy bed with fresh linen, contribute to a feeling of peace. When I set a tray for myself, even if no-one else is going to see it, I like to have matching tableware and a jug of milk rather than the carton. A pretty melamine tray can be easily purchased in a bargain store today. (Isn't it a pity that it is so hard to get plates to match our mugs?)

But that's me. I feel confused and uneasy if the house is in a bit of a state – even if my desk is in a mess. Other people live happily in, for me, a chaotic environment.

The important thing is to have your home in whatever way makes it feel most like home for you. If you keep old newspapers under the cushion of the armchair, and pile up the empty bottles and jam-jars under the stairs with unused jackets, board-games, broken umbrellas and the toaster which gave up three years ago — you have a right to make that choice, I'm not better, just different. There are hoarders and there are discarders.

But if you are uneasy about the state of your home scene, why not plan a make-over for it? There are certain to be nooks and crannies in the house and even in yourself that could do with a new lease of life. Even a new face-cloth and a bright matching nail-brush in the bathroom can make a difference. A couple of sunny tea-towels in the kitchen and a pot of primroses on the window-sill could make you feel more cheery. (But maybe you like the plastic roses?) For as little as five euro you can give your house a gift. A new pair of slippers can make you feel less down-at-heel in yourself.

What I'm thinking about here is the occasional person that lets their house and themselves go to seed *because they have lost heart* in doing anything with it. That's the person I would like to encourage. If your neighbour seems at a low ebb, how can you help to raise her or his spirits? Not by suggesting a spring clean, which could be intrusive and hurtful. But, perhaps, by suggesting a little outing together during which you buy some little thing for your own kitchen saying, 'I'm tired of the old cutlery-holder or the manky tea-towels I have. Do you sometimes feel it would be great to get rid of half the old bits we all hold on to?' Maybe she shrugs with disinterest. The best thing then might be to head off together for the cuppa and be ready to encourage chat along cheering lines. We all need light-hearted chat and a readiness to listen is a great gift. If he or she opens their heart, that's confidential so zip your lips.

I started off by writing about our mixture of dependence and independence. We all need to be free to be ourselves and yet sometimes each of us spots the moment when a neighbour, a friend or a family member can do with the experience of being gently linked. It's a delicate situation, isn't it? We've all met the intefering old so-and-so and we've also longed for the warm-hearted, sensitive person who encourages us to bring new joy into our lives.

Chapter 6

Spring Cleaning

'Talk to yourself in a reassuring and supportive way.'

Self-Esteem by Theresa Francis Cheung

Earlier I wrote a little reflection on 'self-esteem' and a few of the things that might help us to become positive and more confident about ourselves. Have a spirit of adventure in acting on thoughts which might give life a sense of unfolding rather than being a bit 'stuck in a groove'.

If you have a dream the older years may give you time to make it a reality. Stick with it for a little while and turn it around so that the sun of positive reaction can shine on all aspects of it. Why not you? Why not try something completely new? Doreen, an energetic sixty-two-year-old, suddenly got the idea of walking a neighbour's dog when the neighbour was ill. Now Doreen and two friends have set up a little business and are paid for their dog-walking.

Paul no longer has a garden because he is no longer able for all it entails. So he went to a nearby 'show garden' and offered to come in regularly and 'dead-head' flowers. The head gardener is delighted.

But there are things that any one of us can do at home to make us feel better about ourselves. What about getting down to one of those activities that you have put on the long finger for ages. Like what? Well, perhaps your wardrobe needs some culling? Have you kept clothes, or shoes or jewellery that you haven't worn for ages? You may have loads of oldish, comfortable clothes which you like to wear around the house? Possibly you don't bother to change them when you are 'just dropping in next door' or simply running up to the shop for a carton of milk. So, hoping that you won't meet Mrs Bucket, you dash across the road. Mind you, your outfit isn't bad – just a tad frousty – but you don't look smart and you know that. Now you realise a bit guiltily that you have about twenty such outfits. Your good clothes are there too, getting very little fresh air as you wait for a super-duper occasion for wearing the expensive mauve dress or the dainty blouse. Then there's the lovely soft jumper which still has its label on it and the jacket which might stain easily. Oh go on! Be a divil and get rid of half of the 'frousties' and give the newer and newest a bit of an airing. There are plenty of charity shops which are delighted to take older clothes (though not the dregs!). So you'll feel good about helping a charity as well as giving yourself a boost. Into your diary write beside Wednesday: 'Clear out the wardrobe'. Then, be strong and do just that. It may take a couple of attempts to do the job fully – after all there are years of back-log there. But what a relief when it looks roomy rather than cluttered. The same goes for the shoe cupboard... You'll never again wear those strappy black models – so OUT they go. And the hand-bags from the Maggie Thatcher era could find a new life in a charity shop. A good 'clear out' is cleansing to the spirit.

Jewellery is an interesting possession. Whether it is your granny's old necklace, the ring you got when you were twenty, or a piece of costume jewellery, why not wear it? Granny's gift may require you to take out the beautiful mauve dress, so surprise your friends at the next possible outing. The ring you could either wear tomorrow or give to a delighted daughter if it is too small for you. Jewellery never wears out so give yours a chance to shine. Feelings of being a 'new you' will put pep in your step.

A strange aspect of ageism is the way in which older women are discriminated against in shops which favour those in their teens and twenties. Clothing for men is more standard and doesn't change with the seasons. Have the shops not realised that we older women are there in increasing numbers? Retired people can have quite a lot of spare cash and are often searching high up and low down for clothes that suit our stage in life. The fact that we do not have figures like models does not mean we are uninterested in fashion. Firmly and confidently mention this to the department manager. Or, perhaps drop a note to her or him. Older people should be pro-active in expressing their needs; seventy-year-old suffragettes.

CHAPTER 7

DRESSING-GOWN
AND SLIPPERS

'UNFORTUNATELY MANY PEOPLE DO NOT CONSIDER FUN AN IMPORTANT ITEM ON THEIR DAILY AGENDA. FOR ME THAT WAS ALWAYS A HIGH PRIORITY.'

General Chuck Yeager

A cold in the head can make us feel droopy at any age. In our younger years we had little choice but to get up, take the usual cold medication, grab a large handkerchief and get on with the job. The job may have been mothering the family or getting out to work (usually not both). Often the distraction, plus some medication and a few early nights did the trick.

Unfortunately when some people retire they become pre-occupied with illness. Instead of deciding on the usual healthy steps of fresh air – weather permitting – gentle exercise, vitamin C and a tasty meal, they take to the bed for the whole day. (Incidentally, the correct version of a relevant old saying is 'Feed a cold and *stave* a fever'). To settle for a full day in the dressing-gown and slippers can produce a sense of being unwell and we put off doing even the simplest little tasks as a result. So, unless advised otherwise, try to have a refreshing bath or shower and put on easy, relaxing clothes. Give the hair a brisk brush and then survey the scene for the day. If the sun shines you will be more likely to take a notion to go to the corner shop if you did not hang on to the dressing gown all day. A bit of discipline can be well worth exercising because it is so easy for older people to get into a pattern of dressing-gown, slippers and hair like a bird's nest. An occasional dressing-gown day may be a real treat for a person determined not to extend that one day to two or three. Walking is a great exercise to do regularly. I'm not a marathon walker. Even twenty minutes five days a week would be a 'success' for me. This keeps me flexible. Maybe you can do better? Pushing the vacuum cleaner, bending and stretching for housework and going up and down stairs are all good for us (though I have a bungalow!). Mention all this to your doctor so that he or she can assess your particular fitness level for exercise. Isn't it all too easy to excuse ourselves from the discipline of taking regular exercise when we are fit enough? I make weak excuses to escape that discipline. So I'm writing this to myself as well as to you.

Of course it is good to have ready-made jobs and hobbies for yourself at home; things you enjoy doing and will get into even if you are not feeling on top form. (We'll talk about those later.)

That is not to deny that as we grow older we need more rest. A good bed is a great asset – no hills and hollows! You need to be able to get in and out of it at your own easy rate and not to feel that you have to do a high jump in order to hit the mattress. It should be just right for you to sit on and swing your legs on to with ease – and a certain level of grace. Likewise, avoid those 'sinky' chairs which may be comfortable to drop into but can cause posture problems plus the need for a crane to get out of. Settle for a firm upholstered seat at the height which enables you to have both feet on the ground without slumping or stretching.

We must share a little reflection on the importance of keeping the old grey matter from shrinking due to inadequate exercise.

Our intellect needs to be stretched a bit. It can happen that once we are no longer child-rearing or involved in a job outside the home we drift into a narrow local world which contributes little to giving the brain the physical jerks it needs well into our later years. Sometimes we can make an unspoken decision not to take much interest in what is going on in the world because it's all 'a bit grim'. Hey! C'mon! Our prayer for the needs of now will be missed. So it is good to be able to pinpoint needy people, pray, and keep an eye on world progress.

CHAPTER 8

QUIRKY OCCUPATIONS

'THERE WAS NEVER A GREAT CHARACTER WHO DID NOT
SOMETIMES SMASH THE ROUTINE REGULATIONS AND MAKE
NEW ONES FOR HIMSELF.'

Andrew Carnegie, Industrialist

I have enormous admiration for handicapped, crippled, bed-ridden or other house-bound people. Many think up such original things to do with their time. Some even sell their handiwork! The following are a few delightfully quirky and sensible ideas shared with me.

Make simple clothes for a standard doll or teddy, for example a nightdress, skirt, sleeveless top, bow tie, and so on.

Knit good thick bed-socks or day socks for yourself or a friend. For day-socks put anti-skid furniture pads on the soles.

Make a small doll's cradle by lining a plastic fruit-container; a mattress, pillow and coverlet edged with lace (all washable!). Get good at it and sell locally.

Ask a friend to bring you brochures from a craft/games shop to check for a new hobby.

Wood-workers could make stables for Christmas cribs, to be sold locally.

Make little wooden animals from prunings of whitethorn or driftwood. Varnish.

Make up verses or limericks about friends and family and have fun with these when there is a bit of a family gathering. Invite guests to do likewise.

Write verses for all types of greeting cards (birthdays, congratulations, new babies). How about making the whole card with cut-out pictures from papers and magazines? Use card-quality art paper available from stationer's or art shops.

How long is it since you constructed something from matches or made a model plane?

Embroider a corner of your pillow-cover, towel or cushion cover to give it a personal touch. Your initials or a little floral design could be lovely. Do another for a friend.

Sew two large tea-towels together to make a roller-towel for the kitchen.

A simple, small tape recorder is great for recording favourite poems, songs, jokes.

A special white-board (with markers) on which to draw, design, write messages, sketch new plans for the layout of your room.

Adult colouring books, with fine felt markers to colour. I have a lovely one with reproductions of sections of the Book of Kells.

John (a retired carpenter) makes little polished wooden boxes for a deck of cards.

Bill no longer drives, but he saves up the money he would have spent on the car and takes a taxi to a friend or to a museum or art gallery.

How about starting a scrapbook of pictures cut out from papers or magazines? Pat collects pictures of politicians to help him to remember each name, face and job. The message: *Try anything!*

CHAPTER 9

NEW FRIENDS

'OLD AGE AND THE WEAR OF TIME TEACH MANY THINGS.'

Sophocles

ecause it is less usual for men to be left alone in old age we seldom read or hear about how things are for them. I suspect that they could be even more lonely than many single women are. Men are less likely to share such feelings with other men. Those who are widowers could find it hard to create a homely atmosphere wherever they now live. They may not have the home-making skills that women do.

Then there are those who never married, but who, through practice, are able to make the kind of home in which they are perfectly at peace. Of course, when working days are done and the friendly atmosphere of the workplace is past, there can be difficulty in building a new life. Much of what I write about clubs and classes is applicable. Pubs can become home from home.

Priests in parish work come to mind as those who may find old age a particularly lonely time; also priests in communities where there is little warmth. I knew of one community man who told me that when he returned to his community after a week of retreat-giving, there was no welcome. He had simply not been missed. No-one said, 'How did it go?' or 'Glad to see you back'. It must take a lot of strength to fill the gap created by such lack of caring.

I think it must be very helpful when a family welcomes a priest into their home and treats him as one of their own. Needless to say, Fr Tom earns the welcome by not expecting the chair to be dusted for him or lunch to be other than in the kitchen as usual. He helps clear the dishes and really does become one of the family.

Such welcoming parishioners are few and far between. Many a diocesan priest cooks his own chop, microwaves a couple of potatoes and a bit of broccoli and eats alone. Others, I'm told, become great cooks and regularly have a friend or two to join them.

But what of men or women, single, celibate or widowed, who, having retired from active involvement now find themselves with little or no regular companionship?

There are many widows, widowers and single people who would enjoy the companionship of a person they know who might accompany them to a film, for a country drive or who would share a Sunday lunch and relax together looking at a good TV show or play.

The tricky bit is how these friendly people can get together to meet simply as friends. Many would sheer away from placing an ad in a newspaper or responding to one there. We would hesitate because we could be taken for the wrong type of ride. We could find the person far from being compatible and, perhaps, less glossy than the ad made out. Perhaps there would be no common ground for chatting. Needless to say, plans to meet a person for the first time need to be thought out carefully. If each has a car, bring both cars and travel separately. Meet in the lounge of a good hotel. Get a taxi home if you haven't got a car. Perhaps bring a friend along, or meet in a son's or daughter's home. ('I'll be in my daughter's house on Wednesday evening so do drop in there.')

To try the internet might be a better bid, but elderly people are quite often unfamiliar with computers and would hesitate to ask a son or daughter to try it for them. It can be both fun and educational to learn. Internet chat rooms can be dodgy. Exploitation can so easily take place, so do be cautious. When we are lonely we can be vulnerable to the wolves in their attractive sheep's clothing! Even if you choose not to meet people over the internet, it can be helpful in finding out about amenities, clubs, and so on in your area.

One can meet new people through friends; an introductions agency; by attending classes and introducing oneself to people, or by getting an extra cinema or theatre ticket and phoning a person you've been shy to approach saying, 'Care to come?' Go on, chance it!

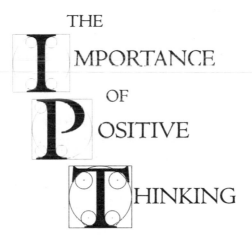

THE
IMPORTANCE
OF
POSITIVE
THINKING

CHAPTER 10

DREAMING

'INSIDE EVERY 70 YEAR OLD THERE'S A 35 YEAR-OLD ASKING "WHAT HAPPENED?"'

Ann Landers, Columnist

The night my hot-water bottle burst was one of those occasions when I resorted to a few choice words that I save for such occasions.

Just ready to get into bed, I had said my prayers, thanked God and made requests for a variety of blessings. With my usual optimistic anticipation of bed, I pulled back the covers. I didn't notice anything until I had stretched my legs down and then that slow realisation... the sheets were sopping. Suddenly my plans were changed. I pulled off the bed-clothes to examine the extent of the damage. Everything was wet. Living alone, I have only one bed. So what next? I couldn't bring myself to 'phone a friend' at 11.30pm. I draped wet bed-clothes around the bedroom, stood the mattress on its side, turned on the heating and headed for the living-room. My pillows, saved from the flood, some cushions, my tartan picnic rug, a dry duvet made up nesting materials on the hearth-rug (my couch is too small). I decided that I would give myself every comfort, so I balanced the little pink table lamp on the fender by the pillows and picked out my favourite 'dream-it-up' travel book. Then I made myself a hot drink and, very deliberately, allowed myself two calorie-laden biscuits.

By then I was smiling. Dreamily, I felt that I was on a visit to a little one-room cabin on the mountain side by Lake Como in Italy. The chilly night air of the lake was all around. But the cabin had absorbed the sunshine of the day and was smelling warmly of pine and resin. My bed on the floor was all any traveller could want. Outside, far below, lay the lake, quiet on the surface, but deep down, teeming with life. Dreamily I wandered up the cobbled street admiring the colourful little shops of all shapes and sizes. I remembered the little cafe where the charming waiter had served me a dish with the wonderful name which sounded vaguely like 'Starletta Rinca' (I know very little Italian).

When I had tried to ask about a dessert, he responded 'Ah, si, si! We haf Crinka Rammel maked 'ere.' Now, what on earth could that be? Daringly, I agreed to try it. Back he came with a little brown earthenware bowl of... wait for it... cream caramel! Crinka Rammel – of course. Delicious in any language.

I was beginning to feel dozy so I thought of the pink sunset and the way in which night falls so suddenly in foreign parts. I turned out my little lamp. As I drifted off to sleep I was imagining my further wanderings in that town where planning permission must have been unknown such were the magical shapes of shops and houses. Even the geraniums followed no rules as they issued forth profusely from cracks in the dry walls. I came to a tiny white church. (Now that I think of it, I had borrowed it from one of the Greek islands!) My imaginings merged with dreams, the little church smelt of burning candles and incense and the floor was wet. I got a sheet to mop up the water. It became glistening white marble.

When the morning sun slid through the gap in my living-room curtains, I had to blink for a moment to consider my whereabouts. My improvised bed was a muddle of cushions and rugs. The pink lamp had slipped into the fireplace. I got up rather gingerly – not being agile any longer – and opened the curtains to a sunny morning in my familiar setting. I offered this new day to God. Before I faced the hot-house of my real bedroom, I made some tea and toast which I enjoyed in the warm rumple of soft furnishings where I'd spent such a happy night. I recalled the words of the Psalm: 'God speaks to His beloved even while they sleep.' Now isn't that a lovely realisation? I must try to go to Lake Como sometime. I've never been there.

CHAPTER 11

TUG OUT THE WEEDS

John 15:9

'hou shalt renew the face of the earth' we pray confidently to the Holy Spirit.

When one is living alone and feeling a bit lonely, it is easy to become introspective. We may blame ourselves for things that went wrong in the past and even the mistaken decision of yesterday. 'If only I hadn't...' can be a sad beginning to a thought process leading to negative and even angry feelings towards ourselves and others. That train of thought needs to be nipped in the bud. It is simply not true that everyone – including oneself – is nasty, mean and unlikeable all the time.

Try immediately to turn your thoughts to the positive. A little walk at that point can be the beginning of refreshment. Exercise sets the positive chemicals rushing to your help. Everyone has made mistakes and misjudgements so you are just human. If you have to stay at home just now, have at hand some music that brightens you up and with which you can hum along. If you are imaginative you may like to put on some light classical music, close your eyes and be transported to the seaside or the mountains where happy thoughts can follow the gentle soaring of the music. Pop music may give you a more bouncy and energetic feeling.

We have to make up our minds to get into positive thinking. Perhaps phone a friend to enquire how he or she is (not, this time, to recount *your* miseries!). Write a little card of 'get-well' wishes or congratulations. Remember someone who is doing an examination or has moved house. There are so many possibilities for well-wishing.

Make a list of your own achievements, happy times, kind deeds, and have it ready to read when you have an attack of negativity. Yes! You have done courageous, funny, kindly and helpful things. Get them all together and thank God for those occasions. Why not ask Him for more of the same.

If you are inclined to feel even a vague anger

or grudge towards somebody or towards a group, the sure-fire way of dealing with that is to forgive and pray for them. That prayer, like a boomerang, comes back to heal oneself, not immediately perhaps, but with perseverance. Even then that person may walk past you, nose in the air. Don't allow her attitude, which contains her personal pain, cause you to deviate from your course of prayer.

If there is a situation which you cannot change, you may well find, as I have found, that the only one you can change is yourself. Talk nicely to yourself about how that change might be expressed; now there's a positive challenge. 'Perhaps I am his problem?' I reflect honestly. Forgiveness has a potent healing effect.

Look into yourself. Ask yourself, 'What's bugging me? Have I just allowed self-pity to take root and flower unobstructedly?' You know the way a weed can choke beautiful plants. It is no good to simply remove the leaves of the weed. We need to dig down deep and haul it out by the roots. This takes time. Ask God for His strength in identifying the weed and tug at the roots with gusto. Today a bit comes out. 'I'm really doing fine', you say. Congratulate yourself.

Tomorrow you'll have another go at it. Throw a few summer seeds into the freshly-dug earth. That digging brings about positive thoughts of the good things that will flourish once the crooked, tenacious old roots are removed and the sun is able to reach the new seedlings.

CHAPTER 12

SMILING IS HEALING

'OLD AGE IS LIKE EVERYTHING ELSE. TO MAKE A SUCCESS OF IT YOU'VE GOT TO START YOUNG.'

Fred Astaire

Did you smile at the above comment? I really want to write about the power of a smile. Age makes no difference to the charm of a smile. Recently I looked at a TV documentary on that inspiring organisation L'Arche. Conceived by Jean Vanier, it began with the formation of a community of wounded people – some were physically disabled, others had disabilities of mind and emotional problems. The carers in the community discovered that each of us has much to learn from people who have different and more difficult challenges in life than we ourselves have. We all share the fact that none of us is perfect so there is room for every human being to blossom. Everyone in L'Arche is both a teacher and a learner in the ways of life.

To help someone else to laugh must be one of the most precious gifts. To see these people smile, play, experience gales of laughter turned my heart to the God who designed that experience for all of us to share. The capacity to share one's highs and lows honestly and freely with others who are spontaneously comforting is to plumb the meaning of compassion. Only God could have thought up the idea of a smile!

One little elderly lady showed up quite often in the programme, participating and interested and with a beautiful smile. The fact that she had few teeth left made no difference to the admiration I felt for her as she recited the final prayer of the programme. Her almost toothless smile filled her face and sent out the message of that prayer with total honesty; her personal belief in a God who smiles, shone through.

That very same week I saw another, more scientific programme on smiling. It seems that, from a distance, a smile is the most easily recognisable facial gesture. By three months a baby responds to a smile – the broader the better – and he or she will take to the smiling person quickly. We never lose that first baby instinct. In that programme there was a series of four enlarged photos of the face of a young man. In each photo he had a different, quite relaxed and pleasant expression on his face – thoughtful, concentrated, relaxed, smiling. Every person, asked in a main street vox pop to select the picture they most liked, chose the smiling face. The vast majority of people do respond with a smile to the smile given to them. It is true, then, to say, 'Smile a while and when you smile, another smiles, and then there are miles and miles of smiles'. With a smile there is an inner transformation in giver and receiver. To smile is a gift given to everyone. Some of us use it too little. Let's change that.

People who have had a great deal of hardship and worry may not feel that there is anything funny in life (though there always is). But the smiling I speak of is not to do with joking or responding to a comedian, it springs from an inner sense of wanting people to feel good. For that reason, I think that we can be sure that Christ smiled very often. Smiling may have been considered so much part of His loving nature that it did not seem necessary to report it. But can you imagine the children crowding around a dour, grim-faced, serious man? Not only did He smile at them, but also at the crowds to whom He told such rich stories. When He healed someone, I can truly imagine His happy smile. So when we talk to Him in prayer, don't forget to smile. Then close your eyes gently and imagine Him smiling back. Isn't that lovely? Pass it on.

Chapter 13

Spirited Initiatives

'If you have faith, nothing shall be impossible.'

Matthew 17:20

Is it possible to get a 'spoil-sport' eighty year old? Indeed it is. One way of spoiling the present for someone five years younger is to moan, 'Wait 'til you're my age. I was fine at your age.' Yet there are people who do that. Not only at eighty, but also at seventy if the person is experiencing difficulties then. And it's not fair to those who are that few years younger. We all have to go through our own particular stages of ageing and we need each other's help and encouragement.

Anyway, not all elderly people who are five years older than you are having a rough time. They may be older in years, but many have a positive frame of mind. I have one friend who is ninety and her outlook is cheery in spite of her very real disabilities. It takes her half the morning to get up. But she never faces a day without a crisp, fresh blouse and her bit of make-up giving a pink glow to her skin; that's her way of lightening up her day. 'Put a good face on and you'll feel more perky', she laughs. I admire her so much. It is a good lesson for all of us, isn't it?

It's worthwhile to be with people who are light-hearted. However house-bound you may be, do play music and listen to audio-tapes and watch TV programmes that cheer you up and keep you in touch with current affairs. We cannot always be light-hearted. Some may have to struggle against all sorts of disabilities and are melancholy by nature. They need the rest of us to visit them and be bringers of good news. It is important to be sympathetic, but also to lessen the emphasis on ill-health. The visitor could prepare by way of collecting some interesting and light-hearted bits of news from newspapers or magazines to share. Even if you have to cut them out, you can say, 'I've collected a couple of things to read to you to get your opinion on'. 'Wait 'til you hear this!' or, 'Does this remind you of anything?' Perhaps a piece about her childhood home-town.

I must tell you about pensioner Sam: Sam was seventy-nine and though partially blind, and arthritic, he continued to look after his garden. The bit he could no longer tend, he prepared with stones and then poured on cement which he levelled out as best he could. Around the irregular edge he 'planted' lovely stones from the local beach, having invited some neighbouring children to help him collect and carry them. He scattered sand on the cement both before and after it had dried and in the centre he set a bird bath. Some artistically gnarled and twisted hawthorn and driftwood provided intermittent sculptures. Then came the 'pièce-de-rèsistance': Sam had made a small, deep hole close to the bird bath. From his daughter's garden dump he resurrected last year's Christmas tree, bereft of its pine needles, but having an artistic tracery of bare branches. He sprayed it with protective varnish and popped the tree into the prepared snug-fitting hole in the cement, filling around it with white stones from the beach. He decorated the tree with an array of hanging birdfoods. Nestled at the centre was a red-roofed bird-house – a detached residence for some lucky family of tits – he hoped. Competing birds hopped around excitedly.

Sam told me that last Christmas he decorated this tree with gold and scarlet weather-proof baubles and the small drifts of frost and snow really beautified it. 'That tree will last five years,' surmised Sam, 'then I'll replace it.' From his kitchen window where he likes to sit, he makes further plans for his little plot of land. At the same time with his knobbly arthritic fingers, he studies the left-over hawthorn pieces from which he shapes little birds and animals – now that's what I call spirit.

Chapter 14

Decision to be Happy

'Never have I enjoyed youth so thoroughly as in my old age.'

George Santayana, Writer

Remember to be happy. Happiness is often *a decision*, just as love is. There are certain ways of behaving which tend to make us feel good.

Ask yourself, 'When was I most happy?' Sometimes happy things may come to your mind in a jumble, some seemingly quite insignificant; for example, one of mine was the joy of having a new leather school satchel. When it was hardly a week old, Jim, who sat beside me, got sick into it. I wept then, but now I smile at that memory. Then with a mental skip I am in a country lane on a hot summer day with a man I loved. I can remember that on one side there was a high bank covered with grass and meadow flowers and on the other side there were fields reaching to the hills. There was a smell of freshly mown hay and warm earth and my heart was turning over in an ecstasy of that sort of feeling that you want to preserve forever. It is just a step from heaven and it is as though we are not allowed to go that step further in this life. A taste, a flavour. Then that laneway tapers off into a mist...

Taking time to notice things and wait on their beauty is an important wisdom. I recall the simple sight of a tiny blue butterfly landing on the cheek of one of my babies. Just that. Fragility met delicacy and trembled there. I almost held my breath and now, in my seventies, I treasure the stillness in which to linger with the feeling of those precious minutes. They provide material for a meditation.

There can be a tinge of melancholy in these thoughts. But it is a bitter-sweet happiness that one wouldn't want to be without. Love-letters were treasured, and in time they got lost or yellowed or turned to dust. Nevertheless the thought that at sometime someone loved me that much, can bring joy mixed with longing. This very mixture is the essence of our being. I write down memories so that I won't erase the sensations of having been young, or having babies (how did I ever cope?). I recall a day of laughter with young friends and some years later the unplanned 'skinny-dip' when I was in my forties. On holiday, my husband and I discovered a tiny, isolated beach and on impulse we dived in and caught the moment. I could describe it as if it were yesterday – the sharp cold of the water, the strange freedom of being naked, embracing under water and coming out to dress, laughing, without a towel to wrap up in. Linger with the memory. Focus on its texture and its cadence. Then try not to follow that by a sense of needing to deny your present age. There's a time for everything... Every day we are creating new memories for the future.

I heard a story of a little girl who asked her grandmother, 'Granny, how old are you?' The granny hesitated and then replied, 'I'm so old that I've forgotten'. 'Well', responded the child, 'if you look at the label on the back of your knickers, that will tell you.' I often wonder what are some people afraid of in hiding their age. It is a sort of denial of yourself. I can understand an actress who at fifty still pretends to be in her thirties – and looks that age. But for the ordinary person I think it's fine to be proud of your advancing years. Most other women have worked it out anyway! Why have we failed to give people an ethos that enables them to see maturity as an asset? By our later years we have acquired a lot of wisdom. We can see through the affectations and poses of the young. We have no need of such artifice. We can be ourselves. I won't try to repeat the old excitements; who would want to give birth or try skinny-dipping in her seventies? But I want to be open to having new experiences. Did you hear of the ninety-six-year-old man who died shortly after a sea-side holiday? A neighbour, on seeing the deceased laid-out, commented, 'He looks beautiful. The holiday done him a power of good'.

CHAPTER 15

POSITIVE RESPONSES

'THE TOTAL SURRENDER PROFESSED BY OUR LIPS TAKES TIME
TO PERMEATE OUR WHOLE LIVES.'

John Dalrymple, 'Simple Prayer' p.73

Some people have planned their retirement carefully and progress placidly into old age. There is the dog to walk, the garden to care for. There are DIY jobs to be done, bingo on Thursdays and church on Sundays. Of course, there is the news on TV and times have clearly changed. But haven't times always changed? The old phone still works and leave it to the kids to grapple with the new technology. Interesting to listen to the youngsters, but leave it at that. Everyone to their own. Yet, such people can feel disturbed when they do not understand the modern lingo, the obscenities. But they shake their heads, let it be and proceed in their measured and chosen way. 'Live and let live', they say as they contribute to needy causes and welcome the neighbours in for a chat. Worry about terrorism, in our own culture and in the world, keeps people in at night and rosary beads are grasped more tightly. Anxiety can peak in darkness and loneliness. We need to be practical about good locks on doors and windows. The gardaí are very helpful in advising about security. If you find yourself particularly anxious, do talk with a good friend and perhaps with your doctor.*

Confiding in an empathetic and listening friend can be a very healing and comforting experience. But a suggestion: decide together on the length of time you will give to this sharing. Then be strict with yourselves and move on to other topics – interesting, funny and newsy. Choose light-hearted books and television programmes. Take exercise in the fresh air.

Elderly people can be positive and responsive to the best that is emerging in our society. I remember visiting a ninety-year-old former teacher, Angela, now arthritic, almost blind and

---

*   There is a Senior Helpline you could call at the cost of a local call. The person there is ready to help you. Phone 1850 440 444. It is strictly confidential. It can be good to talk things through.

a permanent patient in a Dublin hospital. On top of her bedside locker was a piece of paper with her wobbly handwriting slanting from top to bottom of the page. I was asking her if she found the days very long in her confined situation. Her eyes twinkled as she said, 'Let me show you my list'. She indicated the piece of paper which I handed to her. On it were the names of friends and relatives who needed prayer. In addition there were the names of leaders of the Church and State for whom she had decided to pray. Added to that there were peoples of the world who were neglected and marginalised and living in abject poverty. 'I find them all on the news', she said, 'and my job is to take them by the hand individually and bring them up to the throne of God for His mercy, love, healing and forgiveness – or whatever they need. So, in my head, I'm busy all day', she twinkled. At that time I was rushing around like a headless chicken and I recognised my need for her calm and meaningful intercession. 'Will you take me on?' I asked her. 'I'll be your prayer secretary', she said, smiling at me. And she never forgot that promise. Indeed it was a promise that many older people might make to the busy younger folk. Another day I asked her exactly how she did it. She told me, 'It's like living with God. I take time to picture Christ. Then I tell Him everything; open my mind to Him. I remind Him of the needs of people and imagine bringing them into the room to sit beside Him.' Of course, she chatted to visitors and to people around; she listened to the news with her pen and paper balanced in front of her. 'Pain is the great prompter to prayer', she confided one particularly bad day. That's a completely new way of looking at our world today. But what a blessing to be prompted into such fundamentally timeless holiness.

Chapter 16

Beauty and Wrinkles

'One of my greatest delights is that I have out-lived most of the opposition.'

Maggie Kuhn, activist

here's the beauty in old age? Only poets talk like that. Look at me!' concluded Eileen as she pointed her walking stick at me. I jumped back in mock fear and we both laughed. 'At any age beauty has a lot to do with being positive', I commented, 'and isn't it great to have a laugh!'

It is such a pity to allow loss of the smooth skin and curvy figure put us into bad mood. I remember a lovely lady who lived near us when I was first married. She was in her late seventies and she always greeted me with a cheery hello from her window, or tilted an imaginary cup towards her lips with a questioning gesture. Would I like a cuppa? I often went into her and she showed delight each time. The children were never a problem to her. She had such a natural way of chatting to them. She never complained of creaking joints or failing sight though she had both. Her eyes crinkled at the corners of her wrinkled face and I never thought of those crinkles and wrinkles because she was so cheery. Inner beauty comes from a deeper place and it can transform the whole person.

One day she triumphantly took out a book which was familiar to me. It had belonged to her daughter who lived abroad and both the daughter and I would have treated our copies of that book with scant care. It was the Leaving Certificate poetry book of our day. I hadn't seen it for some years. Elsa had often helped her daughter to memorise the necessary poems, 'And now I love it', she said. 'It means so much to me.' When you are not obliged to recite the poetry in class next day, you can let it create new pictures, prompt you to really look at the trees, encourage memories of daffodils and of listening to the sea with a shell cupped to the ear. She picked out a couple of the poems in which her daughter, prompted by the teacher, had underlined evocative words and phrases to be treasured. Some of what she read to me set me off at a gallop of recitation at which we both laughed. I still have my own copy of this book and Elsa's suggestion has reminded me to take it out every so often to do a bit of reciting and remembering.

We have to make decisions about creating contentment in our days as we become less able for the activity of earlier years. Contentment is such a marvellous gift to acquire.

Jenny, another seventy-seven year old, is now crippled with osteoporosis. Of course, it is really hard for her. But sometimes we can adjust old interests to suit our new situations.

Jenny's beloved photograph albums has the old stick-on 'corners' by which to attach the photos. Many of these had become unstuck. So we took out one album and looked at the possibility of re-sticking the photos. Jenny got into trying to name all the old relations, friends and neighbours in the pictures. We decided that a new type of glue would do the trick along with a black marker to fill in names, occasions, and estimated dates. She got interested, busy and her mood changed. Contentment set in.

CHAPTER 17

COURAGE IN ADVERSITY

'YOU MUST NOT SET YOUR HEART ON THINGS TO EAT AND
DRINK; NOR MUST YOU WORRY.'

Luke 12:29-30

hen we are preparing to bake a cake
we bring together all the required
ingredients: flour, eggs, sugar,
baking powder, salt, cherries – and so on. It is
interesting to notice that we would not wish to eat
a spoonful of any one of these ingredients. Yet,
when they are all brought together and
surrounded by warmth, they become a delicious
whole.

Life is a bit like that. The individual
ingredients are not all to our liking, but when
mingled with care, the result can be a triumph of
the human spirit.

An example of this can be seen in the life of
my friend Angela (see page 64). She planned
from the fact of being in fairly constant pain.
Her hands were gnarled and twisted, yet she

could touch and feel beauty. When we touch, the reaction is deep within ourselves. The lovely result of a baby grasping your finger does not depend on the perfection or deformity of your finger. It is an inner experience. This indicates the 'intactness' of the inner world even when the shell we call the body is wounded. It would be such a mistake to let ourselves think that disfigurement of the visible body must alter negatively the contours of the soul. It is from the soul that qualities such as courage, loving kindness and rich thoughts come. Our response to suffering is there too. What a gift to be able, even occasionally to reach deep beyond suffering and draw forth hope. Angela did that habitually: she wished good on everyone. She imagined herself personally presenting a legion of wounded people to God. A smile played readily on her lips. She thought my children were the best of fun. Yet one day as she tried to turn even a little in her bed, she put to me the question, 'Did Christ try to move His body even a little, on the cross?', 'Was he able to scratch the itch of the blood trickling down His face?' All her thoughts seemed to come from a soul made healthy and vibrant by contemplation.

Then there is Pauline. She is partially blind and living alone. 'How do you manage?', I asked her. In her firm, practical way she told me of not allowing any visitor to disturb the positioning of her furniture or kitchen utensils. Her son helped her to get in touch with the section of her local Health Board dealing with the needs of visually-impaired people. They sent a lovely young woman out to Pauline's home. This woman advised, not only on gadgets to simplify life, but also on helpful attitudes. Pauline was excited by the prospect of a collapsible white cane, dark glasses, taped books for the blind, cassettes and CDs. She was already getting the large-print books from the library. The Health Board woman gave her the necessary addresses of suppliers of these accessories as well as the whereabouts of the parish-based meals-on-wheels or, alternatively, WelCare Foods who deliver food to your door.[1] Pauline was assured that help was available if she had further queries.

Pauline had already discovered parish amenities listed by the secretary of her church. She attends a writer's class as she loves to hear the homework of budding authors being read out and discussed. Kind members bring her to and from the venue. Pauline herself offered to talk about blindness to senior pupils in the local school. She described to them the feelings of the blind or partially blind person – what it felt like to walk up their main street. She even recruited a couple of students to do some housework for her.

Pauline faces the main street brandishing her white cane as though separating the waters of the Red Sea. She walks through the crowds smilingly murmuring her thanks. She has to use her feet sensitively as pavements can be rough and uneven in places. She memorises the number of steps into the hotel or up to a friend's hall-door.

And what about shopping? On the back of a large white page of old, used computer paper she scrawls out some of her grocery requirements. Customer Service assured her of the help of an assistant when she came to shop. She chooses a quiet time of day. She exudes the smiling gratitude that draws people to her. The supermarket sees that her bags are delivered to her kitchen.

Is she very lonely? 'Yes, I can be', she responds, 'but so can most sighted people from time to time.' But she doesn't let it 'in on her'. She phones a friend, or listens to an inspiring audio-book. She also dictates taped letters to her family and friends abroad. 'I'm sure I make loads of mistakes with the tapes', she laughs. She also talks with Joe on the phone. He is a young blind man whom she met through friends. 'We enjoy a bit of a moan but don't let that take over.' They empower one another to face the ups and downs. Both have found the richness of silence in which they can hear the rustle of the leaves, the movement of the waves on the beach. The dawn chorus of birds is music to their ears at springtime. She enjoys a drive because she can still see some colours and some changes in the contour of local roads. She tells herself when she is happy so that she won't forget.

Pauline is realistic. She admits that life can be painful but she lets the pain in rather than getting mad or frustrated at it. 'Trying to get things out of our head only gives them more energy. Tears are great cleansers', says Pauline. I remember poems and prayers I learned long ago and nowadays I'm not visually distracted when I say them aloud to myself.' She asks me, 'Did you fully understand the poems and prayers we learnt at school?' And I didn't at the time. 'Well,' says Pauline, 'their meaning is only now dawning on me.' That's great.

Pauline's blindness has exposed her inner depths. What a heroine she is![2]

---

1   (Freephone 0800 773 773 for their brochure)
2   National Council for the Blind of Ireland (NCBI),
    Whitworth Road, Drumcondra, Dublin 9.
    Tel: 01-830 7033/1850 334353.
    Open: Monday to Friday: 9am – 1.00pm, 2.00pm –
    5.00pm

Deafness can also be a problem as we grow older. NAD (National Association for Deaf People), 35 North Frederick Street, Dublin 1, has ten regional units throughout the country. A new service for those experiencing hearing loss is provided by a mobile resource unit initiated by NAD. Through this travelling unit people can have their hearing level assessed. The unit also provides information on a range of services and aids available to people who suffer hearing loss. Included will be information on family support services. Contact NAD on 01-8723800. Perhaps this unit will soon be in your area.

Chapter 18

The Old Guard

'It's not what happens you that matters but how you react to it.'

John Powell

Alice had a tiny suburban flat. There was one tree outside. It was as good as anyone else's tree and the birds that nested there were top-class birds. Alice cleaned and polished her little home and loved to see the early morning sun touch her small oak table in the window, gently investigate her room before disappearing behind the oak leaves.

Alice had three brothers. They didn't really approve of Alice because she had married 'beneath' them. Her Joe had had a different accent. Joe had died three years ago.

Alice liked to have her brothers and their wives in about once a year for Sunday tea. That was a challenge because she was what was called a 'plain cook' and enjoyed simple food – creamy porridge, homemade brown bread, a tasty rasher and egg, biscuits like Fig Rolls and Goldgrain. So what would she give her grand guests?

Not only did the food worry her. But where would she seat them? Six adults plus herself was 'full house' in her little parlour. With the two leaves of the oak table open, it would be almost impossible for them to jostle around as she did in their houses. Oh dear! Why had she invited them so impetuously?

On Saturday Alice went to the supermarket. She looked at food like dips and wraps and baps and goodies with Italian names which her sisters-in-law usually served. Last time she had served ham sandwiches and sausage rolls, but had overheard one of the sisters-in-law whisper, 'sandwiches again'. Possibly a salad? But there was no room for extra plates.

As she wandered around in confusion, a baker lowered a tray of fresh doughnuts onto the shelves. Golden-brown and sparkling with sugar, they smelled delicious. Alice took eight. Further along she saw carrot cake and the 'window-cake' their mother had always loved. She placed one of each in her trolley. A dozen crispy rolls followed. She would butter them with real butter and put egg mayonnaise on half and creamed salmon on the rest. It was all shaping up. Passing the biscuit shelves she saw some chocolate wafers marked 'three extra free'. So she got two packets. She added a packet of Gold Blend tea because the green packet might not be to their taste. Full-cream milk might be best when you didn't know what people usually took. They might think her mean if she got the watery kind.

All aboard and Alice felt she had the menu worked out. She planned to get as much as possible ready on Saturday night so that she wouldn't be too fussed on Sunday.

At home she unpacked the bags. Looking at the doughnuts she was assailed by doubt. The boys had liked these when they were children at home, but now? Her doubts became so strong that she donned her raincoat and clutching the unopened bag of doughnuts she ran for the bus. Sitting gazing out she thought, 'Whatever about exchanging a pair of shoes, I can't face the girl at the check-out with a bag of doughnuts, can I?' She tightened her jaw and sat up straight. 'I'll try' said Alice.

The supercilious-looking girl at the check-out got Alice to repeat her request twice. 'Show me your receipt', she said sharply. Alice had forgotten to bring it. 'Sorry', replied the girl arrogantly. Alice walked towards the exit, surreptitiously leaving the bag of doughnuts on a shelf as she passed. Her confidence wilted.

That evening she got the room set up. She had pulled the table out so far that the couch and her armchair now crouched together to the left of the fireplace.

On Sunday morning she went to early Mass. After eating her porridge and tea she wrote herself a list of the items she had to prepare. The rolls had lost their crispness so she gave them a few minutes in the oven. Butter. Maybe they take the low-cholestrol kind? She banished that thought as she draped mother's lace-edged cloth over the table. It looked lovely. Alice unearthed cake plates, serviettes and her mother's tea-set which she hoped they'd all remember fondly. She covered the food with cling-film just as her sisters-in-law would do.

After enjoying a bowl of soup she lay down on her bed for forty winks. Then the finishing touches. At four the phone rang. One of the couples had a call to make en route and would be late. 'Never mind', responded Alice casually.

When the first couple arrived she nervously explained the seating arrangements. (Had her brothers put on weight, she wondered, or had her chairs shrunk?) By 5.15 they had all arrived. Alice was wearing her flowery two-piece. To her amazement, the 'girls', both deeply tanned wore jeans and shirts, one with heavy gold chains, the other with impossibly high-heeled sandals. Their blonde-streaked hair was carefully careless, their leather handbags looked expensive. One brought Alice some deli jam, another brought a pair of those little socks with plastic blobs on the sole and the third laughed merrily as she said, 'I've come with one arm as long as the other!'

Alice manoeuvred her way to the kitchen. She knew that in their homes there would have been 'little drinkies' first, but she firmly put the kettle on. Unveiling the rolls she discovered that, buttered and filled, they had again lost their crispness. 'Can we help?' chirruped the girls. But there was no room for helpers.

Three-quarters of all that Alice had prepared went uneaten. Two slices of window-cake and one of carrot cake were disposed of. The rolls must have been unappetising and the pyramid of biscuits was treated like an ornament. The boys talked politics and the girls shrieked with laughter. Alice gave little laughs and small, unheard political interventions. (Had the clock stopped? she wondered). By 7.30, they had left.

Having cleared the debris into the kitchen to be dealt with later, Alice made her little willow-pattern pot of tea, put it on a tray with a small pile of leftovers, donned the socks with the plastic blobs and almost fell into her cosy armchair. 'This', sighed Alice 'is luxury, and I can have it every day.' She added, 'And deli jam for tomorrow'. But Alice, what about being true to yourself next time?

CHAPTER 19

YOUR LIFE STORY

'YOU ARE PRECIOUS IN MY EYES AND HONOURED AND I LOVE YOU.'

Isaiah 43:1-4

What attitudes have you towards ageing? Your hope of feeling good today can depend on your attitude, hidden or expressed, about growing old. Society does not help older people to feel good about ourselves. Old-fashioned respect is not expressed in many situations to people of any age today. So we really need to have respect for ourselves. Don't allow a gaggle of school-children push you off the footpath or cause you to flatten yourself against the wall to allow them bundle past. Stand firm, smile, say 'excuse me' and hold your ground. This is a metaphor for the determination we should have as society tends to write us off. Determine to live life to the full, to walk tall and value yourself as a treasure that will never be available on earth again once you step across the horizon. Yes! You are that: a unique, once-off creation.

See your life as a story you are writing from day to day. What will this character (you) do next? Give him or her a light-hearted part to play in this chapter to contrast with the shadows of the last chapter. Even if the shadows linger, set yourself up today to be happy. Be generous enough to get excited by other people's adventures. Even if you are not part of their excitement it will be good to have a bird's eye view of it (perhaps by phone or letter). It all adds to your story. It is possible for the older person to find within him or herself the heart of a child where fun and frolics still liven up the imagination. Encourage your sense of humour. I bought a book of jokes once, ones that give me a happy giggle. And I taught myself to laugh out loud at some of the best of them. A sense of humour can differ from person to person, but it is the greatest asset to be ready and able to laugh at oneself. For example: why am I getting so uptight about Florrie's bad manners? I'm not going to let *my* reactions be dictated by her. Anyway, the kernel of that problem – snobbery – would make an amusing incident in my book of life if I decided to see it in an amusing way. We may need to lighten up! Act happy, act pleased and these feelings become real.

Older people can find their world narrowed by their retirement, by friends dying and because of less physical energy. Imagine one chapter of your story dealing with the habit some 'oldies' fall into: gossiping to create entertainment and gain attention. Local chatter is good to share but sour scandal and detraction can be destructive. In your story, put that scandal-giver into a chapter where she can see the reflection of herself as she really is. Reflect and reproduce a remembered gossip session.

As we grow older, friends become ill and die. There is grief and loss and we can feel so diminished by having to say 'Goodbye' and move on. It is important to celebrate even while we feel the natural sense of loss. Isn't it great that Pat was such a courageous, warm-hearted and positive person — so much to bring to the eternal world. Even at the funeral, but also afterwards, try to be ready to give the family of the deceased friend a real sense of your affection for their loved one. For example, do not murmur the usual 'Sorry for your trouble' which is so trite a way of expressing something that moves your heart. Gently touch the hand or cheek of the relative and say with real warmth, 'Pat meant so very much to all of us.' 'You had such a lovely Gran', you might say smilingly to a grandchild.

While naturally missing your friend do not settle for dragging along sadly from one monotonous day to the next without planning to change routine. Make a surprise of this chapter of life. What will tomorrow's page bring? 'The Lord makes all things new'. Great!

RESPONDING TO CHANGE

CHAPTER 20

CHANGING TIMES

'WHEN I WAS YOUNG THERE WAS NO RESPECT FOR THE
YOUNG AND NOW THAT I'M OLD THERE IS NO RESPECT FOR
THE OLD. I MISSED OUT COMING AND GOING.'

J.B. Priestley

Older people can feel threatened and dismayed by the changes in our society. 'It's all screwed-up' declared Minnie when she had spent an evening with grown-up grandchildren and their parents. She felt an overwhelming anxiety at the attitudes they expressed, their casual manners, their status symbols and even their dress. She had been looking forward to the family party, but when she arrived home she felt exhausted and stressed.

A grandad was invited by his son for a family drive into the hills for a Sunday afternoon treat. When he came home he was clearly dismayed by the behaviour of the twelve- and fifteen-year-olds in the back of the car. They argued over their mobile phones and yawned loudly from time to time, claiming to be bored. When their father stopped the car and suggested to them that they be quiet and enjoy the wonderful scenery as spring unfolded all around them, the older lad said cheekily, 'We've seen fields and mountains before, dad, so what's new?' Grandad squirmed in his seat. He was sad for his grandchildren. Could it be that they were no longer capable of responding to natural beauty? Living on a merry-go-round, music pounding, stress level always raised, pressured by exams, can render mundane the peace, contemplation and faithful repetitions of nature. The grandfather thought of himself at their age, when, as a boy with his dog, he used to go for long hikes and do his bit on the farm.

I think it is a pity if we allow the stress and secularisation of aspects of contemporary culture destroy our peace of mind. But having been brought up in the pre-1950s Ireland, we cannot help looking over our shoulders at the old, seemingly predictable Ireland where there was a sense of the sacred, a feel for the poetic, an exaggerated bowing to authority amongst an 'easy-going' people who respected the good things as 'blessings' rather than 'luck' and confidently left the key in the hall-door when they strolled up to the shop.

But was it *all* good? There were many people sunk in poverty. Education was the privilege of the few. Women were second-class citizens in the eyes of controlling husbands, a triumphant Church and burgeoning State. A very un-Christian attitude was fostered between Protestants and Catholics. Guilt and fear were felt by many Christians as notions of sin and hell were emphasised and love and forgiveness seldom preached. Children were reprimanded for expressing opinions and few were taught how to face the secular world thinking for themselves.

Perhaps in those innocent years we did not recognise that we had a crisis on hand? Ireland was largely Catholic and insular and we did not have the impact of sophisticated media to inform us of events around the world. Abuses of every kind took place but were either concealed or unknown. Now everything is being opened up and challenged. Boundaries are being removed. We need to move slowly. Suppose that in a football game all rules were removed except that the blue team scored at one end and the red team at the other end. What would the mid-field game be like? Again, suppose all rules of the road were withdrawn. There would be even more chaos than we already have. Clearly, we need moral, civil and family rules and boundaries.

Women have won equality with men. Both need to grapple with children's rights. Clearly, for a time, we are going to have a much smaller Church-going percentage. But the participants are likely to be people who have made clear-headed, informed decisions about their participation in the Church. Church leaders at every level, lay and religious and of both sexes, will humbly listen and work with heart and head towards the coming of God's kingdom. 'Remember I shall make all things new', promised God.

CHAPTER 21

AMAZING CHANGES

'ONE OF THE ODDEST THINGS ABOUT LIFE, I THINK, IS THE
THINGS ONE REMEMBERS.'

Agatha Christie

here have been numerous amazing
accounts of changes that have taken
place in society within the lives of
those born in the 1930s and 40s.
Has there ever been a generation which has
experienced such upheaval in the way people
live? Here I have taken from different lists a
selection which will surprise many of us, make
us laugh and give youngsters pause for thought!
Be ready for questions from the grandchildren
such as, 'Granny, what did you *do* when there
was no telly?' and, 'Grandad, what do you mean
when you say that you *pushed* the mower?' And
to both the grandparents the question, 'How
do you mean – *discipline*?'

Signs of the Times

A Grey Panther (senior citizen) is one who was here before the Pill, television, frozen foods, credit cards and ball-point pens. We were around before penicillin, polio shots, contact lenses, videos, Playstations; before dishwashers, tumble-dryers, electric blankets, air-conditioning, drip-dry clothes and panty-hose ('nylons'). Santa filled stockings not sacks. Tooth-fairies were rare and the value they put on a tooth was a 'thrupenny bit'. ('A what?' today's kids will ask.)

We got married before we lived together (how quaint can you be?). We thought that 'fast food' was what you ate in Lent, a 'Big Mac' was an over-sized raincoat. 'Time-sharing' meant togetherness. Disposable nappies meant the child had entered the pants' stage. A 'chip' was a fried potato or a sliver of wood. Hardware meant nuts and bolts and software wasn't a word. A mouse in the office ate crumbs and lived behind the skirting boards. Girls wore 'Peter Pan' collars and cleavage was something butchers did. We never heard of FM radio, tape decks, internet, computers or 'dot com forward slash'. Mobile phones and text messages were unknown. Men never wore earrings and a 'stud' was something that fastened a collar to a shirt. 'Elastic waist and knee' described women's knickers. 'Denims' wasn't a word. 'Getting off' referred to dismounting from the tram. 'Going all the way' meant staying on the bus until it reached its terminus. 'Cool' referred to chilly.

In our day 'grass' was mown, a 'joint' was a piece of meat and 'pot' was something you cooked it in. Cigarette smoking was fashionable, 'coke' was a form of fuel for the kitchen range. 'Farm-fresh' food really was just that. A 'gay' person was the life and soul of the party and AIDS meant helpful supports for handicapped persons.

***

We are today's Senior Citizens – a hardy bunch when you consider the way in which the world has changed and the adjustments we have had to make. By the grace of God, we have survived, and the time has come to sit back and decide whether or not we were the lucky ones...

'History repeats itself', they say. So hold on to this document and see which terms your grandchildren will understand in twenty years' time. The likelihood is that they will have a whole new set of 'Signs of the Times'.

CHAPTER 22

RELATING TO THE YOUNG

'I AM UNDERSTANDING... WHOEVER FINDS ME FINDS LIFE.'

Proverbs 8-14:35

Enjoying adult children and grandchildren entails thinking a bit about your relating with them, your expectations, your hang-ups and their needs from you. They live in a world where there is no coherent set of beliefs, no discernable boundaries or fences. They are struggling to find a Truth they can depend on. They need you to:

- Love them, and pray for them.
- Be there for them.
- Invite them to visit or arrange to meet for lunch.
- Think through negative attitudes you may have towards youth today.
- Work out the 'why' of your own standards.
- Seek what is valid in their lives.

- Respect them and where they are in life.
- Encourage them to tell you about themselves.
- Listen non-judgementally to what they have to say.
- Treat them with courtesy.
- Do not be destructive or angry about topics.
- Seek to know what jobs and interests involve them. Their future plans.
- Learn how to be a calming influence.
- Ask him/her to explain phenomena like 'peer pressure' or 'bullying' as he/she sees it.
- Tell them what you're reading and ask, 'What about you?'
- Try to avoid saying too often, 'When I was your age...' (All too easy!)
- Ask them why they think so many kids complain of boredom.
- Put out a feeler to check their interest in current news issues.
- Ask her/him to explain, simply and slowly, about the internet, texting, etc.
- Remember to ask about a current boy/girlfriend and friends in general.
- Get them to tell you about sports they follow and who they see as being role models.
- If there is an area of failure, encourage them to keep trying.

- Respond to their questions about your life/health in as positive way as you can.
- 'How are you, Gran?' Respond, 'Toddling, love' with a smile. (Not a lengthy account.)
- Don't make it all heavy-going. Share a laugh.
- Show appreciation for a visit, a gift. 'Do come again, even for a quick visit.'
- Suggest they might phone you before coming in case you go out or need a nap.
- If one of them sends a holiday postcard, remember a 'Thank you'.
- Keep their interests in mind and take a relevant cutting from a paper or magazine for them.
- This often means jotting down their interests in your 'Memory Book.' We can quite easily forget!
- 'I think differently, dear. But we can still talk about it'. Then don't get stroppy.
- Don't break rules the parents have made. Yet, in your home let your standards hold.
- If they're staying too long simply say, 'I'll have to let you go. I have to do...'
- A warm hug, 'You've made my day'.

Our young people are precious. Sometimes their tastes, activities and way of life are very different from our experiences. Individually, any of us finds it hard to achieve a fully coherent personality. They're only starting. So imagine that young people who come to you have a little card pinned to their baggy jackets, reading, 'Delicate, handle with care'.

Chapter 23

What Others Do?

'I STILL HAVE TWO ABIDING PASSIONS. ONE IS MY MODEL RAILWAY, THE OTHER — WOMEN. BUT AT THE AGE OF 89 I FIND I'M GETTING JUST A LITTLE TOO OLD FOR MODEL RAILWAYS.'

Pierre Monteux

Did you ever question things beginning with the phrase, 'I wonder if other people...' followed by an assortment of questions such as '...feel uninteresting as I do?', '...don't have a shower every day?', '...miss having sex?', '...give as a gift an unwanted present they received?', '...re-use teabags?', '...polish their shoes on the edge of the stair-carpet?', '...pin up their hem rather than sewing it?' Usually such self-questioning is about such personal little thoughts and habits.

I assure you that many people have such secret minor and major thoughts. So, you are nice and normal! There is something endearing about the fact that we all tend to have hidden ways of breaking the rules which mother made for us long ago. She still 'sits on our shoulders' giving our hair a little tweak when we take naughty short-cuts. I often hope that, even in my absence, I'm not giving those 'tweaks' too often to my own grown-up family. ('Put it away; don't just push it under the bed.' Oh dear! I can hear myself.)

It's comforting to know that probably the majority take short-cuts or have funny ways of being economical such as putting the left-over rasher in the fridge for a tomorrow that never comes. We may even feel afraid that the neighbours will find out. Perhaps you don't ever let people see you without your mask of make-up?

It's a pity to take ourselves too seriously. If the producer of a play asked you to play your part more light-heartedly and coolly, you would probably make the change without hesitation. So, give yourself the freedom to have a giggle about yourself. Overly-correct people also have their problems. There is much un-examined pressure which may well come from childhood or the need for social approval. They, too, may not allow all those little human touches emerge. I feel that as we grow older we gain the wisdom to laugh together with our friends at all our little foibles.

It is a bit sad to see 'mutton dressed up as lamb'. Anyway, an ageing face can have much character, and serenity. Old people can make others feel comfortable. Yet body image may continue to be a source of anxiety. Everyone accepts, objectively, that wrinkles appear as the years progress. Call them 'laughter-lines' and make light of this change. Somehow weight can get transferred from the face and neck to the stomach or hips! We can either become disheartened or decide to do a few positive things to keep ourselves fit and healthy according to the stage in life we have reached. We can plan interesting things to do, thank God with a smile for all the things that are okay with us. But do see the doctor if you feel unduly depressed, tired or need some advice about nutrition. There are times when a visit to a sympathetic GP can mark a distinct change in our attitude to ourselves. It's healthy to claim our funny little behaviours and share them with a close friend of two.

At any age either a man or a woman can miss having sex — if one has remained single, if a partner is no longer interested, or a spouse has died. Many people enjoy sex into their late years — particularly women. As men age, some find that they cannot achieve regular or full erections as in younger years. This can cause a deep sense of loss and they hesitate to get close for fear of another disappointment. Women too may experience discomfort during sex. Talk to your partner and to the GP about those conditions. Mature people do not emphasise orgasm as an end in itself. Remember that the closeness of an embrace can be a great comfort to both people. Don't let the warmth of a tender hug be lost. Assure your partner that a cuddle is a very special sharing Closeness can mean so many things to people who love.

Chapter 24

Brown Envelopes

'AGEING SEEMS TO BE THE ONLY AVAILABLE WAY TO LIVE A LONG LIFE.'

Daniel-Francois Espirit Auber

Getting older means different things to different people. A lot depends on one's genetic pre-disposition, one's health through the years, the wear and tear one has experienced and, possibly, any chronic ailments that may have pulled one down. We cannot put a chronological age on the occurrence of changes that are quite natural at different stages in the ageing process.

But, for all of us, it seems to be a good idea to develop orderly habits and cut down on clutter as we reach the later years. Clutter in the house can cause clutter in the mind. 'Where did I put the letter about my pension? I thought I'd left it behind the clock.' The clock has got pushed out nearer to the edge of the mantlepiece because of all the bills and receipts that have been pushed behind it. A few simple files would ease the situation so much. One might be labelled 'Bills' and another 'Receipts'. Further divisions could be 'Electricity', 'Doctor', 'Tax', 'Household', 'Bank' and so on according to how much detail you want to go into. Then have all these files in one place and as soon as you have read your post, deal with what needs immediate attention and file away the rest. You will be so glad to have done that. Even if you do not want to deal today with all those piles of printed matter, you could start the files with this weeks mail and gradually sort out little bits of the accumulated, yellowing bills, notifications, receipts and 'bumph' that comes with the mail. You'll enjoy the feeling of having sorted it all out. Have a wastepaper bin close to hand.

There are other orderly habits that are well worth a bit of determined organisation. You may have a hook in the hall for your keys – but they have seldom found their way onto the hook. So you have found yourself having a frantic search just as you are ready to go out. This week you can start the discipline of putting the keys on the hook as soon as you come in. Just for the present, tie a big red ribbon to the hook so that you'll see it as soon as you come in — one person tied a carrot to the hook so that he had a laugh as soon as he entered the hall. Be firm with yourself: KEYS ON HOOK.

Thinking may get more slow as we progress into our later years. You come to the check-out in the supermarket; you are packing your bag when the girl says, 'That's nineteen euro, twenty-three cent'. The next customer edges into position. You stop packing away the purchases and fumble for your purse. But your handbag is choc-a-bloc with all sorts of stuff which begins to fall out onto the counter. The check-out person continues to hold out her hand and yawns. You get fussed and confused with the coins and notes; the next customer towers over you. Self-confidence drains away. Calm, calm. Take a deep breath and go at it quietly. It's only a matter of minutes. Smile at the girl and say, 'Thanks for your patience'. She may begin to be more of a help. Act cool. Don't go at it as though you were under a slave-master. Whew! It's over — but will the experience repeat itself next week? Can you do anything to avoid that? Wouldn't a minimalist approach to the handbag be a good start? Right! Once home, empty it all out on your table and get rid of the junk. Before you go shopping next, have a clear idea what notes you have and put the itsy-bitsy coins in a box on your dresser for some good cause. 'Clutter-free' is a state of mind but it also takes a bit of pre-planning. Don't carry much cash. Just use your basic credit card.

This kind of calming can take place in all areas of our lives. It's never too early to start. What about today?

CHAPTER 25

BUSINESS PHONE CALLS

'OUR GREATEST GLORY IS NOT IN NEVER FALLING, BUT IN RISING EVERY TIME WE FALL.'

Confucius 551–479 BC

M ags wanted to make a phone call about a mix-up regarding her insurance. Two 'indecipherable-to-her' letters had arrived within two weeks. So she decided to talk with that nice young man who had been in the office when she called there two years ago. Frank, wasn't it? She put the two letters on top of the books on the phone-table, sat down and dialled. An anonymous voice as though from a science-fiction TV programme started to speak: 'If you want blah blah, press one; if you want blah blah, press two; if you want ...' Oh dear. Mags simply wanted Frank and she couldn't speak to this sepulchral voice. She put down the receiver. 'What do I want?' She decided that it could be 'Bills'. Off she went again. Eventually, with her blood pressure rising with the anxiety, she got a real person. She explained her problem and was invited to 'Hold on, please'. She was then treated to a recording of 'Danny Boy' for three minutes. She had given up all hope of finding Frank. Finally a male voice said, 'Accounts. William speaking. Can I help?' 'Yes', replied Mags. 'My bill seems to be wrong.' William responded with, 'What's your name, address and account number, please?'. Mags gave her name, address and almost her old phone number, but corrected this quickly. 'Account number?', said William. Mags fumbled for the letter and reached for her reading glasses. 'Where would that be on the letter?' she asked with rising anxiety. She longed for the kindly Frank she had met at the counter. On went the seemingly relentless quiz.

All phone calls come to an end in some way. At the conclusion of this one Mags didn't feel at all sure that she had received a clear reply to her question. (Ask confidently for *clarification by letter* if you feel that you need such.) But William was going to write. Mags lay down on her bed. Beside her on the floor were the two letters. Forty minutes had passed.

Mags, it could happen to a bishop if he were in his seventies. So what do we learn from such calls? Firstly, in modern business phoning, you are liable to get that 'if you want such-and-such press one' and so on. So, before you phone, read the two letters calmly and jot down what you want to ask. Then underline in red pen things like your account number, date of last communication, name of the person who wrote to you, department if stated and any other numerical mysteries given. Be familiar with the layout of the letter. If you feel really mixed-up, write out your query so that you are ready. Be as specific as you can be. Business people simply do not often seem to understand our language so we have to allow for that. Don't let yourself feel inferior. William is supposed to be your assistant. He probably couldn't boil an egg when in his flat. Visualise him in his pyjamas burning his breakfast toast.

Sometimes our underlying problem when we try to sort out some aspect of our finances is that our whole financial situation is in a bit of a mess. It is a vague sort of nightmare to those who may not have managed this aspect of their lives before losing their money-handling partner. Basically it is important to keep the business letters tidy and sorted. We may need the help of a financial planner. The bank could advise you about such help. But since an accountant or financial advisor may ask you for your papers, have them as ready as you can. Try not to give him or her a shoe-box full of dusty financial 'things' all mixed up like a brown stew. That's the advantage of having a budget of weekly expenditure and sorting and filing the rest as you go along.

CHAPTER 26

SELF-ESTEEM

rust me! I've over-cooked the meat again. Silly ass!

Self-esteem is all about how you think of yourself. As we get older the mind tends to slow down. Perhaps familiar topics such as the subject a teacher taught for years, seem to stand up quite well to challenge. That same teacher may find him or herself slow at understanding some new technology, or forgetting the name of a prominent politician. It doesn't help our self-esteem to begin forgetting like this. I find it a comfort to know that many – not all – other seventy-plus-year-olds do likewise. We tend not to be as quick on recall as we once were. I've opened a little notebook for myself which I call 'Memory Aids'. In it I list the names of politicians who are in the news. It includes the names of restaurants I've enjoyed, friend's grandchildrens' names and odds and ends which I may like to remember next month or next year.

Asked about the importance of 'self-esteem' in our lives I reflected on my own experience and found that my self-esteem is quite high in some areas but yet it is low in other ways. Talking with a group of people I discovered that a considerable number of us share similar lapses in self-esteem. Room for improvements there!

Adolescents also lack self-esteem at times. Their appearance is very important to them and a few spots on the face can spell disaster. Likewise, clothes that do not meet some hidden peer standard can cause the young lad or girl to shrink almost visibly and wish the party was over. Self-confidence is just another aspect of being alive that we may need to work on no matter what age-group we are. But let's get at it with a sense of humour. Actually, the person who is cock-sure of himself is not necessarily going to be the popular one. I feel more at ease with the person who whispers to me that he has forgotten the name of the hostess, or that she dreads being asked to perform at a party. 'Fellow-feeling makes us wondrous kind' – or should.

We can be more unkind to ourselves than we would dream of being to another person. I've heard my own wry and unkind self-criticism: 'Silly ass...' 'What are you like!...' 'Typical', 'There I go again – stupid', 'Why can I do nothing right?' These are mild examples of the way in which we put ourselves down. Yet I am a beloved child of God. I am as He created me, so when I insult myself I am being critical of the unique person He designed me to be. I should rather open my arms and give myself a comforting hug. Another thing I have learned to do is to smile at myself in the mirror. Then I put on my sour face; that shows me the value of a smile.

Many of my generation were brought up without being given much praise or admiration. It was thought that we might get what was called 'a swelled head' if we were praised and admired. Now, as older folk, we could remind ourselves of all that we have achieved and of how we can reflect the Father's love for others by our expressed appreciation of them. Heart-feelings need to be put into words more often. We can overlook our vocation or calling to be God's mouth-pieces of encouragement and love to others. Being reeds through which the Spirit can blow is a mighty calling, possible for most elderly people, overlooked by too many of us. Open to the Spirit, we grow to the optimum of our potential. So it is sad when we omit giving the compliment or the hug we could so easily give – especially to ourselves. Up we get and try again!

CHAPTER 27

LIVING THE NATURAL SPAN

'PEOPLE ALWAYS ASK ME WHAT DEATH IS LIKE. I TELL THEM
IT IS GLORIOUS. IT IS THE EASIEST THING THEY WILL EVER
DO... LIFE IS HARD. LIFE IS A STRUGGLE...'

Elizabeth Kübler-Ross, Psychiatrist

I have wondered why, in today's world, some of those in authority seek to terminate the lives of unborn babies and lengthen, unnaturally, the lives of the elderly. I looked up the *Catechism of the Catholic Church* to see what is written there about this matter. On page 491, under the heading 'Euthanasia' I read the following: 'Direct euthanasia consists in putting an end to the lives of handicapped, sick or dying persons. It is morally unacceptable.' It continues: 'However, discontinuing medical procedures that are burdensome, dangerous, extraordinary or disproportionate to the expected outcome can be legitimate; it is the refusal of "over-zealous" treatment. Here one does not will to cause death; one's inability to impede it is merely accepted. The decisions should be made by the patient, if he or she is competent and able or, if not, by those legally entitled to act for the patient, whose reasonable will and legitimate interests must always be respected.'

Continuing to quote from the *Catechism*:

> The use of pain-killers to alleviate the sufferings of the dying, even at the risk of shortening their days, can be morally in conformity with human dignity, if death is not willed as either an end or a means, but only foreseen and tolerated as inevitable. Palliative care is a special form of disinterested charity. As such it should be encouraged.

I had to read that a couple of times and found it to be necessarily stiff in its legalistic language, but yet offering merciful possibilities to the patient who is finding the treatment 'burdensome' and beyond the usual or necessary. I have wondered about the 'over-zealous' medic who may try to keep the elderly, terminally-ill person alive with innovative therapies and cocktails of drugs which may prolong life but offer no *quality of life*.

Sometimes patients and their relatives feel over-awed and believe they have no right to speak. The Irish Society for Quality and Safety in Healthcare (ISQSH) recently produced a booklet encouraging patients to play a much greater role as managers of their own health. It includes questions you may wish, at any stage of illness, to ask the professionals who are looking after you. They include:

- Can you tell me more about my condition?
- Do you have any information I can take away with me?
- Why do I need to have this particular test?
- Are there other treatments for this condition?
- What are the risks of treatment?
- What is likely to happen if I don't have this treatment?

The booklet tells us that 'major changes are taking place in the nature of social and professional relationships.' We have a right and a responsibility to ask our doctors about our medical condition. 'It is no longer acceptable for doctors, no matter how senior, to talk down to patients.' At last we can feel empowered to discuss our condition with those in the medical profession.

I actually look forward to death – though not to the process of dying. It is the assurance of resurrection that has given life its deep meaning for me. If you think that there is no after-life, well, you may be in for a wonderful surprise.

Like the trapeze artist, I hope to make that last jump in faith that Waiting Arms will receive me safely. The drama of life in this world is completed and the rejoicing begins.

CHAPTER 28

A STAGE OF GRIEVING

'UNLESS A WHEAT GRAIN FALLS IN THE GROUND AND DIES, IT WILL REMAIN ONLY A WHEAT GRAIN.'

John 12:24

here is a little poem by Joan Pomfret (Lancashire) which will touch many widows at a certain stage of their grieving. It is entitled 'The Little Things':

> It is the little things that hurt the most —
> Not the long years of marriage
> Loving and giving, now you have left me,
> But the smell of toast
> And all the tender little things of living.
> The fence you mended and your apple tree,
> Your book laid down, your pipe. The unread letter —
> An empty house and no one there to see

If I can cope, or if I could do better!
These are the little things that bring the tears;
But we had love – and still in bleak December
Left all alone after the golden years
I have love still and so much to remember
But oh! The empty chair! The stories told!
My fear of loneliness and growing old,
And all my funny little memories!
But we shall meet again some day, I know, so please
Don't sigh for me – I'll try to end my days
As other widows do, my promise keeping –
It's just the little things
That set me weeping!

Spiritual awareness seems to me to be such a gift in the midst of the loneliness of bereavement. It gives us strength to start our new journey. This is a journey seldom planned beforehand. Part of it entails the gentle alteration of one's attitude to all those 'tender little things' of which Joan writes. Allow them to become blessings in a way we may never have realised in the ordinariness of life before. They can become a treasured part of our inheritance – blessed ghosts of a loved one who is never totally gone.

In time such memories may no longer give rise to tears. But neither have they been banished by tightly closed eyes and a firm refusal not to look back. They have simply faded gently, taking on the quality of a scent that gradually loses its fragrance.

In the early months or years of grief, it can help to sit in the room so tenderly shared and allow the tears to flow. Ask the Father to be quietly there for you, to fill your aloneness with a sense of His presence. Your loved one is so close to God now that a sense of spiritual companionship begins to seep into these deeply personal moments. The 'fear of loneliness and growing old' recedes as the tide moves out leaving a beach washed clean.

Characteristic of grief is the fact that every so often the tide again sweeps in over the rocks. But think of it as a re-cleansing flow just as you come to think of your own weeping as a gift which lifts tension and brings a sense of purification. The God of tears longs to dry your eyes and gradually clear your vision, enabling you to find new purpose, peace and spiritual companionship in the flow of life's tide.

If you are a person who had an unhappy marriage, don't castigate yourself when you feel relief after your partner's death. All can be well now, and you can leave behind you those difficult times and start afresh.

Single people have all the same feelings about the death of a person who has been significant in their lives. We all need comforting when 'the little things set us weeping'.

CHAPTER 29

A NEW HOME?

'DO NOT BE AFRAID NOR DISCOURAGED, FOR I, THE LORD YOUR GOD, AM WITH YOU WHEREVER YOU GO.'

Joshua 1:9

Perhaps you are feeling that the house you're living in has become too big and too hard to keep for your present needs? Many elderly people reach that point. The house, and perhaps, garden too, have become a drain on your energy. It can be a great relief for an older person, and indeed, their family, when we decide to move on. True, there are memories tied up in the present house. These have to be balanced against the fact that it no longer meets one's present needs. Grown-up children may feel that they have to keep a parent's home as well as their own. That's a drain on their energies and perhaps on finances too. But do feel free in making your decision while taking the family views into account.

Smaller houses can feel so comfortable. A flat may be the answer, possibly a nursing home is required? Your local Health Board can furnish you with a list of nursing homes. Interestingly, only 5 to 7 per cent of elderly people are in nursing homes or homes for the elderly. Many care for themselves or have visiting help. A retirement complex can offer security and independence with either individual small homes or apartments. These can be purchased or rented. Calmly write down the pros and cons for different possibilities. Some people long to have no stairs, others don't mind, looking on them as exercise. They are aware that in a few years a stair-lift may become necessary. Have a clear look at your finances. Get it all down on paper.

Some people decide on a 'granny flat' attached to the residence of a relative; others divide a small house between themselves and a friend. Talk with your doctor who has a clear idea of what you may be best able for.

If, for example, a 'granny flat' is a possibility, look at it from every angle. Check out exactly what accommodation it will have. Consider what storage, cooking, laundry, airing and heating facilities it might have. Is there a clothes-line in the garden? Any little fenced-off spot in which to sit outside undisturbed, in good weather (without grand-children, with their natural exuberance, being on top of you!) Be tactful but forthright in exploring thoroughly what expectations of you may be 'built into' your relative's plans. For example, regular baby-sitting may be expected; certain sharing of family meals may or may not be offered. Clarify with good humour. Sometimes the elderly person can be hurt at not being invited to family social events 'after all I'm part of the household.' This can be a delicate situation. Be sensible and realise that a seventy-five-year-old will not necessarily fit in with the fifty-something's guests and may find the children's parties a sore trial! I've heard of a grandparent simply arriving at a social event, presuming him or herself to be automatically expected. Watch out not to be 'stroppy' if not invited and not to be critical if we are asked in and it is not all to our liking. Privacy must be respected both ways and, however loving the relationship, it makes sense to have honest sharing and a written agreement on all aspects of the arrangement.

If you are offered a bed-sitting-room in the home of a relative, it could be a very happy arrangement. But that, too, requires that it be considered from every viewpoint. It is wise to try it out for a month or so before both parties make their decision. Consider the level of independence available and the need for tact in asking for certain arrangements. Sometimes we get on really well with a relative at a little distance, but are thoroughly irritated by each other if constantly under the same roof. Consider the possibility from each other's viewpoints. Share a laugh if it does not seem feasible after a trial. It is not a bad thing to be incompatible. Again, let each write out their hopes and expectations. Boundaries, once decided, need to be carefully observed. Both parties take off their rose-coloured spectacles however fond they are of each other. It may be wise to have looked at homes for the elderly before rushing into a decision.*

---

* The Family Life Centre, St Brigid's Parish, Cabinteely, Dublin 18, has published a booklet entitled, 'Caring Options for Older People'. It lists a wide range of services, organisations etc. Many details are for the East Coast Area Health Board but are relevant to people in other areas of Ireland. It costs €7 including postage from above address. Well worth getting.

CHAPTER 30

MAYBE A NURSING HOME?

'THE LORD HIMSELF WILL LEAD YOU AND BE WITH YOU, SO
DO NOT LOSE COURAGE OR BE AFRAID.'

Deuteronomy 31:8

It is a good idea to think from time to time in terms of the possibility of having to go to a long-stay nursing home. We can pray about it and ask God to give His blessing to that time should it come about. We also familiarise ourselves with the fact that it can be a safe and calm place to be. A lot depends on our attitude of acceptance to the reality of how well we are able to manage in our present situation. Think of it early on. In that way we can build up abandonment to whatever has to be.

The local Health Board can supply a list of registered homes for the elderly. Get the list and, in discussion with your financial advisor (family or professional) discover what you can afford when you have released any assets you may have.

Get a statement from the Health Board as to what allowances are available in your particular situation. There are homes offering medical and nursing facilities and others that offer care and security without nursing.

Make an appointment to have an interview in any home of your choice (and within your means). Bring with you a list of your questions. We sometimes forget our questions in the pressure of an interview. On your visit, ask to have a look around. If this is not possible on that day, arrange it for a more convenient date. This preview is essential so don't be put off by a dismissive staff member.

On your walk around, note what the residents are doing. Do most of them look happy and relaxed? Are there some recreational facilities? Is there any notice up indicating planned outings or indoor events for residents? Is there a garden with little nooks and quiet seats? Are there single bedrooms (ask to see one), or are the bedrooms ward-style? Is the home clean and well-kept? Are there hidden extra expenses not noted in the brochure? Is there a place in which to entertain a visitor or family group? Will you be stuck with a TV in a communal sitting-room or is there also a quiet sitting area? If you can have a single bedroom, may you bring some little pieces of your own furniture and a picture or two from your home? Is there a chapel or meditation room? Are there shops at walking distance for those who are mobile? These are questions that occur to *me*. You may have special ones of your own. Each nursing home will have its own brochure so get one of these from any home you visit and mull it over.

Do not allow yourself to be rushed into a decision. But when your doctor and the family have talked with you, do not put the decision off for too long. Often there is a waiting list in the homes. Pray for the guidance of the Holy Spirit. Do remember that no accommodation will be perfect so try to accept minor hitches.

Some people dread going into a long-term nursing home. Others are pragmatic, have explored other possibilities and realise that it is the only realistic response to their particular health and social situation. I know that I pray *already* for faith and courage should I have to go into a nursing home as a person who can no longer take care of myself. I would insist on having my little crucifix on my bedside locker, my most inspiring book nearby and my rosary to hold; (it is my favourite lullaby when I am trying to sleep). Then try to be a saint! It may be the last chance we'll get for that!

TRUSTING IN GOD'S PLAN

CHAPTER 31

FAN THE EMBERS

'THE CENTRAL NEUROSIS OF OUR TIME IS EMPTINESS'.

Carl Jung

What is known as an 'identity crisis' doesn't only occur at adolescence. The question, 'Who am I now?' can occur at the time of any major change in life. It is very often asked by people who are about to retire from their long-time job outside the home, or by a parent when the last bird has flown the nest. It is asked by widows and widowers, by someone whose life has been utterly changed by a debilitating illness. 'Have I any value now?' can be a cry of despair resulting from the personal experience of extreme loss of one's power or even loss of old, familiar routines. One grandmother said to me, 'All these years since Jack died, I've collected grandchildren from school, brought them home, given them lunch and got the homework started. Now they have reached their teens and no longer need me.' Even at seventy-five such an identity crisis can occur. We must be prepared to re-build our lives. Through the prophet Jeremiah (29:11) God said to His people, 'I know the plans I have for you; plans for good and not for evil'. Adult re-birth is an entry into a strange, new life and there can be a time of pain before this new birth takes place. In the interim, which may be puzzling and sad, recall those words of Jeremiah and turn urgently to God, asking, 'Father, what plan have You prepared for me now?' Then be as calm as possible, prepared to wait and think and pray.

I remember a day when I asked God that question. I followed the question by telling Him what I *didn't* want Him to call me to do. Quite quickly I realised that I must be totally open to what comes about. He will 'fit the burden to the back'. The wisdom of long experience teaches us to wait and pray, tuned-in to even the smallest whisper of a suggestion. Value stillness before God. From time to time I have thought of an involvement at which I rushed. It didn't work out. We need to do some spiritual discernment.

Only by trying might we discover if the light in a particular endeavour has been switched on by God, or if it is a spark generated solely by one's own flash of enthusiasm. As one who has had 'flashes' which didn't come to fruition, I know it's best that prayer accompany an inspiration or a trial run of a seemingly 'bright idea'. Efforts made to re-energise our lives in the way in which we hope God wants, are never total failures. To have tried is, in itself, a learning. Simply to *be* in peace and gratitude may be the plan for now.

Pray to the Holy Spirit to fan to a flame any possibilities for developing the life left to you according to the Master plan. A spark can ignite any material. Sometimes the old and dry material is the best in which to start a conflagration.

The elderly Simeon in the temple waited long to see the child, Emmanuel. He did not have an identity crisis in the waiting. Neither did Anna, the prophetess, who had served and prayed all her life. She, too, saw the Light of the world in her late years. They seem to have been ordinary, retired people, prayerful and hopeful. Eventually, they saw what mattered most.

Chapter 32

A Reason to Live

'Believe that life is worth living and your belief will help create the fact.'

William James (1842–1910)

I was delighted to see how positive and happy Marie was when we meet two years after Henry's death. She had worked her way through grief. Friends and family had been concerned and caring. Marie was, by nature, positive, extrovert and courageous.

She had already been secretary of the bowling club and the members were wonderfully supportive. Having lived in that suburb for fifteen years, she and Henry knew a great number of people there. One had called with an apple-pie, another with a flask of home-made soup and they sat with her and allowed her share her sadness, helping her gently to regain her emotional strength.

Marie is a clever woman, well-to-do, generous and robustly healthy. She is a keen gardener and a founder member of the local Women's Club. She loves to travel and this year (her seventy-fifth) she and a friend joined a group heading for a Baltic holiday. So there were a lot of factors in her personality and blessings in her life contributing to her well-being. Such a person weathers well the potential loneliness of living on her own.

The friend with whom she went abroad is a single woman who has a successful nursing career and has taken part-time jobs while adjusting to retirement. She still takes an occasional patient under her wing and teaches in the local First Aid group. Both she and Marie never miss an opportunity to share a giggle or a good belly-laugh. And that is a really healthy thing to do. It also draws other people to share with the jolly one. Remember: 'Laugh and the world laughs with you. Weep and you weep alone. For the world can do with your laughter; it has sorrows enough of its own.'

Some people are light-hearted and sociable by nature. Marie is also sensitive to those who are more introvert and quiet. Each type reaches out to the other as best they can. Elizabeth Kübler-Ross wrote:

There are dreams of love, life and adventure in all of us. But some of us are also sadly filled with reasons why we shouldn't try. These reasons seem to protect us, but in truth, they imprison us. They hold life at a distance. Life will be over sooner than we think. If we have bikes to ride and people to love, now is the time.

It matters so much to have a reason for living. Recently I read a story told by the actress Ruby Dee, which illustrates this fact:

A group of Jews were escaping from the Nazis. They were walking over a mountain, and they carried with them the sick and the old and the children. A lot of the old people fell by the wayside and said 'I'm a burden; go on without me'. They were told, 'The mothers need respite, so instead of just sitting there and dying, would you take the babies and walk as far as you can?' Once the old people got the babies close to their bosom and started walking, they all went over the mountain. They had a reason to live.

A reason to live. Sometimes there seems to be

no rhyme or reason in a world where everyone claims to have their own truth and 'fairness' seems to be to let each one go along with his or her personal belief. For such people there is no objective truth. For some there is no apparent reason to live.

Love was the reason for the people to live in Ruby's story. We can all resonate with the truth in that. Indeed, when life has taught us that love is our 'raison d'être' and we hear St John's words: 'God *is* Love'; that is all we really need to know. Boundaries become established: we do not kill, we do not steal, we do not commit adultery or other crimes, because these are against love. No bullying, no scandal, no injustice. Thus have boundaries been established. So, when there seems to be many choices, we measure them in terms of the loving thing to do. Often we get no thanks for making the loving choice. It can be difficult to stand out alone. But our act of love is our lived response to God. Then, as with those people trudging up the hill, we can be hope-filled even when we are surrounded by an alien environment. 'I am the Way, the Truth and the Life' promised Jesus. He is objective Truth.

CHAPTER 33

IN REVERENCE AND WONDER

'LET NOT YOUR HEART BE TROUBLED.'

John 14:27

remember when I was in Confirmation class the phrase 'Fear of the Lord' came across strongly to me for the first time. At that stage of life there can be quite a few things that one feels afraid of — like a bad school report, an angry teacher, losing one's friend, facing up to the bully. But I did not feel the least fear of the Lord and I couldn't understand why anyone else would feel that fear unless they had done something very bad. Even then, He was my Best Friend so I felt sure that He would understand whatever it was. I put aside the notion of such a fear.

Much later in life I came across people who felt scrupulous about many things because they thought that God would be hard on them if they were not perfect. These people saw God as a Father who was waiting to catch His children in wrong-doing and was ready to punish them. The concept of sin was a preoccupation with them. The unconditional love and mercy of our Father was not an ever-present, comforting awareness. Certainly, sin is a reality but 'perfect love drives out all fear' so let's concentrate on loving and rejoice in the warmth of being loved.

When we are in the later years of life we need to think a great deal about the love of the Father towards whom we are journeying with increasing excitement. So it seems to me to be a good idea to be ever on the look-out for the signs of God's love — through people, through nature, through the blessings we encounter in such unnoticed things as a warm and comfortable bed, clean water, enough food and those little personal blessings that we may have become accustomed to. We are really so blessed. Every time we offer thanks, do caring deeds, we are adding to the health and goodness of the entire universe.

The opposite is to think of God as a domestic pet whom we could control; this is altogether too casual an approach. The truth is that God is beyond all our imaginings, awesome, mighty, just, all-knowing. But in God's great love, this Parent-of-all-parents translated 'Self' into human terms and came amongst us to show us, at our level of understanding, what the Omnipotent God requires of us. In human terms Jesus came to exemplify what God wants of us. Jesus was 'like us in all things but sin'. He, too, was tempted, just as I am. In forgiving, as in all other aspects of human life, He reflects the love of God. Only those who are deliberately doing serious wrong, need fear Him. And even with them He shows mercy. 'Sin no more', He said to the adulteress as He reached out to help her up. And on the Cross the words: 'Father, forgive them for they do not know what they do.'

I used to love the headmistress in school. I was in awe of her. I knew her to be just and I knew that she would punish our wrong-doings. We knew the rules and if we chose to flaunt them, this good woman gave us whatever was the fitting punishment. She continued to love us and do all she could for us. Because we had experienced her kindness and justice, we admired her, but in a positive sense we feared her when we got up to our tricks! I think that

'Fear of the Lord' is to be understood in like manner.

As we draw nearer to death, we realise that, just as emotional and physical pain were part of Jesus' experience, so they are a temporary part of ours. But we know, through faith, that we have a Hand to hold, an Invisible Companion who will be there to lead us across the horizon to that place where fear and pain will be no more.

Chapter 34

Welcoming solitude

'WE ARE FOR THE MOST PART MORE LONELY WHEN WE GO
ABROAD AMONG MEN THAN WHEN WE STAY IN OUR
CHAMBERS.'

Henry David Thoreau (1817-1862)

Do you sometimes feel lonely? I do. To feel that way is not something to be ashamed of. Rather might we see it as a prompting in two directions. The first direction is towards planning ways out of that condition and, strangely, the second approach is to learn to translate some of the loneliness into solitude. Gerard Hughes, SJ, wrote, 'The most lonely are those who are unable or unwilling to face solitude.' The true human situation is that everyone experiences existential loneliness in this life because we were born unique and for union with God.

On other pages I write about the possibilities of socialising and planning activities. But here I want to share what I have learnt to be the richness of allowing solitude. When we befriend solitude it is found to be an enriching and educating experience in any life. Often it is the place in which we meet God most deeply. We need to dispose ourselves towards having that experience. We need to examine what we are calling our 'loneliness' before we rush into claiming how dreadful it is. Why did Jesus go off alone in the middle of His hectic life? He knew how necessary *solitude* is. It could be that we are experiencing loneliness because we over-estimated the power of marriage, money talk or social success to wipe out loneliness for all time. Such expectations were not in line with human experience. We should not expect human beings, even close friends, to fulfil all our needs for talk, activity or even quiet presence.

Therefore, when we are overcome by the immediate pain and grief of losing a companion or a fortune or of finding that people never fully understand us, we can gradually come to know another relationship which is a spiritual experience: the experience of giving time in quiet and stillness, to getting to intuit God in the stillness; spirit to Spirit. We need that deeper answer to the seeming problem of loneliness. Simply allow things to *be*.

The discovery of the gem at the heart of loneliness does not mean that we become overly reclusive. We are in the world so it is healthy for us to be part of what is going on there. The secret is to enrich ourselves by the spiritual discovery of solitude's gifts. It is more than merely possible to become content with solitude. It is a rich reality which enhances our capacity to be listeners when we meet others. Our home can be filled with the companionship of the loving Spirit which we absorb in stillness, silence and awe simply by sitting from time to time where, for example, Mary (the sister of Lazarus) sat – at the feet of Jesus, giving time to listen.

Do you remember when Elijah spent the night in a cave waiting in hope for Yahweh; Yahweh did not come in the mighty wind that shattered the rocks; He did not come, as Elijah expected, in the earthquake nor in the fire that followed. But after all that disturbance of the elements, there came a 'gentle breeze' and it was in it that Elijah heard God. (Kings 19:9-13)

Not for one moment do I suggest that in the discovery of such a 'gentle breeze' and the possible Voice within it, will life become perfect.

Not so. But just as in every other part of life there are the moments of fulfilment and the times of waiting. There are those times when solitude is filled with the inner and outer wind and earthquake experienced by Elijah. The very fact of ever having experienced the gentle breeze filled with the voice of God lets us know what is possible. Something of the peaceful Spirit of God lingers on wherever people watch and wait in prayer.

Chapter 35

God's Word

'Earth's crammed with heaven'

Elizabeth Barret-Browning
(1806-1861)

> 'God loved us first, He spoke first too.
> And He continues to speak.
> He only says one word, it is enough, it will do
> Because His word is Jesus
> Who is everything and the only thing
> The Father has to say.'

J.P. Whelan

Read that over again, aloud. Read it slowly. We are told in St John's Gospel, 'In the beginning was The Word and the Word was with God and the Word was God'. The Word was God's means of communication. God translated His word into human terms in Jesus.

Jesus was to Be and to communicate the Father's message to us. 'This is my Beloved Son. Listen to him.' So we look and listen and try to follow what is today, relevant as it was during Jesus' life, the counter-cultural message of God.

An aspect of this revelation seldom reflected upon is the importance of speaking the name of Jesus with honour and respect. Perhaps as we grow older and more reflective we will have the courage to gently remind people of those words, 'I have a message here that I want you to bring out into the world... Please do not use the Name of Jesus casually' then have those words written out on one of those inspirational little cards (have a few ready to hand out). The world needs that message of life. Oh yes! I know that you may think, 'My grandchildren aren't interested in such things.' But we never know when the Holy Spirit will touch any of us. Even if that young person picks up that message, one other person will have received it.

Reverence was characteristic of the early Christian: reverence for life; reverence for death; reverence for old age, reverence for the wisdom of God. The books of Proverbs and Sirach in the Bible present us with collections of sayings of the wise. These we fully respect. Reverence means respectful awe. We see reverence in the practising members of all world religions. Why do Christians in our country so readily tolerate the irreverent use of the name of Jesus?

There is a lack of respect and delicacy in our society even in the smallest things: if a flower falls in the street many will trample it underfoot. But there are still those people, sensitive to beauty, who will pick it up, perhaps wear it jauntily in their lapel, perhaps place it in a crevice in the wall, maybe bring it home and put it in an egg-cup on the kitchen window-sill. These are people who honour beauty.

Old people, who have honoured God over many years and developed sensitivity to the beauty of creation can sit for long periods of time in the park or by the sea or in their own little garden and reverence there the reflections of God's creativity. Looking at the Chelsea Flower Show on TV is like observing a triumphant choir raising its voice to God. 'I praise You for what You have done...' Elderly people often acquire the wisdom to admire only what is lastingly beautiful. Having seen what is fashionable in the current marketplace, they settle for the on-going gifts of God which are given so faithfully by The Creator.

Perhaps we need to start as early as possible in

life (yet it's never too late) to learn the good habits of respect, reverence, gratitude and sweet temper. Easily pleased and wisely uncomplicated, old people are a joy to be with as are small children.

Read again the words of Christ: 'I bless you Father for hiding these things from the learned and clever and revealing them to mere children. Yes, Father, for that is what it pleased You to do.' (Luke 10:21) And later in that chapter of Luke's gospel (10:23-24): 'Happy the eyes that see what you see, for I tell you that many prophets and kings wanted to see what you see and never saw it; to hear what you hear and never heard it.'

CHAPTER 36

KEEPING A JOURNAL

'WRITE IT ON YOUR HEART THAT EVERY DAY IS THE BEST
DAY OF THE YEAR.'

Ralph Waldo Emerson (1803-1882)

D id you ever hear of journalling? It is a really interesting and on-going occupation. Yet it is not unduly demanding. Goethe wrote, 'Whatever you think you can do, or believe you can do, begin it, because action has magic, grace and power in it.'

What journalling amounts to is keeping a record of key things that are happening in your outer and inner life. Rather than being like a diary in which the entry may be 'Thursday: 11.30 am. Dentist 4 pm. Call on Jane', with journalling you write a bit each day about what you felt and thought. To start with you might write, 'Before the dentist I felt my usual nervous feeling. I wonder why because dentists today do not hurt as when I was a child...' In journalling you can work out the 'whys' of your initial feelings, fears, hopes, etc. Even if you do not think of yourself as a writer, if you start simply you may find the idea of journalling to be fascinating.

Your inner journey is often brought into focus by journalling. We are travelling towards God and learning the route: there are roads that we take that bring us nearer to Him. In our journal we can reflect at the end of the day on moments of grace we were given and thank the Father for these. What we might have called 'luck' we may, on reflection, see and note to have been a blessing. We can also tease out the 'why' behind certain kinds of behaviours of ours during the day. 'Why did I blow-up when Edna suggested the meeting?', 'What made me feel so good when Tom recognised me?' Express our thanks for all the good things — big and small — that happened to us; moments of encouragement, a lifting of a worry, an insight which enabled us to console or be consoled. In our journal we record items when they are fresh and recognise what is being done for us. A worry or fear that has been nagging us may be worked out or put into perspective in the writing of it. Thank God when you feel encouraged and listened to. Spill out your heart, your journal is a very private account of day-to-day living and reflecting.

Occasionally I like to enter a quotation that has helped or touched me, a thought that seems to have been specially given. A photo or a touching picture from a magazine or newspaper can be stuck into the journal. There are places, outdoor or indoors, which give me special feelings of peace. I like to describe those places so that, re-reading this little journal will help me to sense again the serenity of that place and be grateful. What happens to me when I'm praying is another interesting matter to examine in this writing of our most intimate reality. Occasionally a confusing situation or project can be shared with God through the pages of our journal and even clarified by the very fact of writing it down. Note sensitively all God is doing in our lives. Pause at times in the writing. The Father may have something to say.

Your journalling takes shape according to what you find to be interesting and helpful to record. All you need is a one-day-per-page diary or a fat, hard-backed exercise book. Enter the date if it is not already printed in your book.

Then you may write as much or as little as you feel inspired to do. Perhaps you'll skip occasional dates and, instead, stick in a picture, family photo, poem or quotation that attracted you. Maybe you'd like to write in a little note about that? Your personal form of journalling will evolve as you get into the habit of writing up the significant factors, serious or light-hearted, in your journey through the world of God. He loves us in all our humanity and we do not have to struggle with fine words when we are communicating intimately with Him.

CHAPTER 37

SHEPHERDING

'ANYONE WHO ENTERS THROUGH ME WILL BE SAFE.'

John 10:9-10

'I am the Good Shepherd'. I love that image of Christ. His contemporaries would have been aware of all the aspects of shepherding which have been lost to us over the centuries.

It seems that in Israel at the time of Jesus, the shepherd who was despised as the most lowly had skills which were born of experience, and expertise by which he made himself known to his flock.

One example of this which I heard recently is the following: A lamb was often born with what seemed to be a natural tendency to roam and separate itself from the flock. If such an adventurous lamb broke a leg, the shepherd set and bound it. While healing was taking place, the lamb was unable to romp for some time and had to be carried by the shepherd until the limb strengthened. By the time the leg was strong again, a transformation had taken place: the lamb had bonded closely with the man who had carried him and now had no inclination to stray.

Isn't that a beautiful illustration of how God uses our waywardness and straying and pain to draw us to Himself. He binds our broken-ness and carries us. 'I am the Good Shepherd'.

Another piece of shepherding lore is the revelation that there was no gate on the sheepfold into which the sheep were herded for the night. The shepherd stretched himself to sleep across the gap. Thus the sheep would not stray nor be attacked nor stolen without the instant knowledge of the shepherd. 'I am the gate of the sheepfold', said Jesus. Not until I was told that story did I understand the significance of those words.

These are simple tales of ways that are gone. The parables often contain deeper messages than we understand unless the full wisdom is revealed to us.

Jesus spoke so that everyone would understand. He was not only on a four-minute Sunday morning platform. He sat on the steps of the temple, walked the streets and marketplace, ventured into fields, up mountains and down to the lakeside. He would not have made His language difficult nor his thoughts too intricate for everybody to understand. Yet in each of His stories lie depths to be penetrated more deeply as the hearer becomes more enlightened.

I think that the ageing person can do no better than develop the discipline of reading the Gospel slowly, thoughtfully, imaginatively and prayerfully. Isn't it a bit like how we should chew our food — thoroughly and slowly, in order to be able to digest it well.

I have bought myself individual copies of the four Gospels. These little books are lighter to handle, the print is somewhat clearer and I do not feel that there is too much for me to work my way through — a chapter at a time. 'Hasten slowly', I tell myself. In the golden years there is time to savour and explore the Gospels — possibly with a good friend. Just watch what happens when you actually 'feel' yourself into the scene portrayed there.

If there is a course entitled 'Lectio Divina' available in your parish, try it out. Its objective is to bring the gospels more alive for people. There you will meet others who are also searching for deeper understanding of the Gospels. A priest leader will explain and encourage response.

CHAPTER 38

BEFRIENDING DEATH

'DO NOT BE AFRAID FOR I HAVE REDEEMED YOU, YOU ARE MINE.'

Isaiah 43

'Befriend death', suggests Henri Nouwen. Think quietly about death before serious illness actually strikes. While we are still quite well is a good time to familiarise ourselves with that inevitable challenge.

Do you see life as a positive movement towards full union with the Source of our Being? The seed that falls into the earth at burial will spring to life again in a form wonderful beyond imagining. I do not want to think of dying with romantic images or pie-in-the-sky levity. Dying is the final and most tremendous challenge and as we grow older we can become more aware that, in a sense, the process is happening to us every day. It makes good sense to befriend death during life.

For me, part of facing death is to try to live now with sensitive awareness of the mercy and goodness of God. Jesus Christ was God's exemplar of how life should be lived. He was not spared the sufferings that are a familiar part of life for all of us. He also rejoiced at the gifts the Father bestowed.

When we look at the mystery of the life and death of Christ we note that in His final agony, Christ cried out 'Why?'. But because of His having lived in tune with The Father He was ultimately able to trust the Father's wisdom and love. 'Not my will, but Yours be done'. This is an ideal that I struggle to take on board for myself. I pray now that I will be able to echo Christ's abandonment to the Father. It must all have been a mystery to Christ too.

Pray now for the people who may then be close to you, looking after you, holding your hand as you become passive in the face of the inevitable. May those people be blessed with compassion, courage, faith and love, reflecting the Spirit of God to me as I struggle with dying as I struggled with birth. Is this a re-birth into an existence of unimaginable joy? I hope, I hope...

Perhaps I shall be alone for long hours, trembling on the edge of the unknown? I pray now for the courage and trust I shall need should that occasion of powerlessness arise. Will I really be alone or will the trust in God, developed through life, allow me to touch the hem of His Garment at that moment of need? I try now in life to develop such an automatic turning to Him that I shall do so instinctively as life ebbs away. My prayer is that I remain faithful. It is all too easy to doubt.

For many of us it is not what happens after death that is the problem but what the actual process of dying might do to us. When I am, as Teilhard de Chardin wrote, 'passive in the hands of the Great Unknown Forces that have formed me' will I be able to 'treat my death as an act of communion...'? Fr de Chardin prays, 'O God, grant that I may understand that it is You who are painfully parting the fibres of my being in order to penetrate to the very marrow of my substance and bear me away within Yourself.' (*Le Milieu Divin* by Fr Teilhard de Chardin, SJ)*

Now is the time to prepare 'when the signs of age begin to mark my body (and still more when

---

* Fontana Books, p.89

they begin to touch my mind); when the ill that is to diminish me or carry me off, strikes from without or is born within me; when the painful moment comes in which I suddenly awaken to the fact that 'I am ill or growing old...' then the time is ripe to live love more fully and venture forward on the strength of God's word.

CHAPTER 39

HEAVEN AT LAST

'EYE HATH NOT SEEN NOR EAR HEARD, NOR HAS IT
ENTERED INTO PEOPLE'S MINDS, WHAT GOD HAS PREPARED
FOR THOSE WHO LOVE HIM.'

I Corinthians 2:6-9

People often ask one another: 'What do you think heaven will be like?' They wonder in what form our loved ones will meet us; whether or not a pet dog or cat will be there and how God will look! Few will go for the winged angel sitting on a cloud playing the harp!

Our wonderings are no more than human meanderings. We humans are capable only of imagining things the component parts of which we have seen in life: a spotted sunset or a striped rose (we have seen roses, spots, sunset and stripes). But life beyond death is unimaginable to us. For me, one of the finest poetic descriptions of the next life was written by Evangeline Paterson (Dublin 1929). We close our eyes in death: 'And that will be heaven':

And that will be heaven at last
The first unclouded seeing
To stand like the sunflower
Turned full face to the sun
Drenched with light, the Still Centre
Held, while circling planets
Hum with utter joy
Seeing and knowing at last,
In every particle seen and known;
And not turning away again
Never turning away again.

Life is an evolution of the person towards
heaven. We are given just the right time in our
earthly span to develop the spirit of goodness,
reflecting our Creator. It makes sense to me to
imagine that the soul breaks forth from the
body as a butterfly from a chrysalis and soars to
be united with its source as a sliver of metal
races for the magnet.

I wonder if the speed of that travel depends
on the quality of God-likeness of the person?
To journey slowly could be the meaning of
purgatory: having seen God and yet being
unable to race into His arms, slowed by a web
of our own earthly making.

It is all such a mystery, isn't it? So much the better if, in our pondering in life, we become more and more committed to learning goodness and love. When St Paul reflects on love he says, 'Now I know in part; then I shall understand fully, even as I have been fully understood.'

Life after death... Preaching in St Patrick's Cathedral Armagh, the late Cardinal Conway reminisced that as a child he had thought that Christmas was the greatest feast... 'But as one gets older', he continued, 'ones sees that point. The Resurrection is the visible demonstration that there is a life after death, and that is the only thing that can make sense of human existence.'

'Unless there is a life after death' he went on 'this life is absurd. It mocks our deepest longings with its brevity.' On another topic he pointed out, 'One of the most striking things about the past decade is the way in which the myth has been exploded that affluence can satisfy the human soul. The atheist, Camus, was more logical when he said that life was absurd, as indeed, on atheistic terms, it is. It is the Resurrection of Christ, and all that it implies, that is the real source of human hope', the Cardinal added.

There are years spent seeking ephemeral things in life, hoping for empty things, thinking non-essentials to be essential. Buried under a mountain of distractions and possessions, we may have been unable to see the essence of life.

As we grow older we achieve the wisdom to strip life of non-essentials and allow the spirit of things to shine through. Now, perhaps even in pain, we are emancipated by the simplicity and truth that all we really need is to let go in love and to Love. All else is gloriously dispensable.